Asa Hull

Songs of the Golden

A Collection of original and selected songs for the Sunday school and young

people's meetings

Asa Hull

Songs of the Golden
A Collection of original and selected songs for the Sunday school and young people's meetings

ISBN/EAN: 9783337265380

Printed in Europe, USA, Canada, Australia, Japan

Cover: Foto ©Lupo / pixelio.de

More available books at **www.hansebooks.com**

SONGS OF THE GOLDEN.

A COLLECTION OF

ORIGINAL AND SELECTED SONGS

FOR THE

Sunday School and Young People's Meetings.

EDITED BY

ASA HULL,

AUTHOR AND PUBLISHER OF SUNDAY SCHOOL MUSIC BOOKS, PROGRAMMES FOR CHRISTMAS,
EASTER, CHILDREN'S DAY, HARVEST HOME, THANKSGIVING, ETC.

———⸕⸔———

NEW YORK:
Published by ASA HULL, 132 Nassau Street.

CHICAGO:	SAN FRANCISCO:
LYON & HEALY.	AM. TRACT SOCIETY.

FOR SALE BY MUSIC DEALERS AND BOOKSELLERS GENERALLY.

COPYRIGHT, 1896, BY ASA HULL.

PREFACE.

SONGS OF THE GOLDEN was suggested as the title of this book by the many references in the hymns to "Gold" and the "Golden," such as the "Golden Shore," "Gates of Gold," "Streets of Gold," "Golden Harps," "Golden Bells," "Golden Doors," "Streets all Golden," "Jerusalem the Golden," etc. Most of these being titles of songs, gives it significance as a general title.

In selecting the songs for this book, the needs of Sunday Schools have been kept in mind, and we are confident that something appropriate for each lesson during the year can herein be found. Many of the songs are arranged as Solo and Chorus, but the intention is to have the solo sung by the whole school in unison, or as semi-chorus by a part of the school, when it is inconvenient to have it sung as a solo. Some of the songs have small notes which can be sung by the alto, making soprano and alto a duet, but when not thus used they are to be played by the instrument to make full harmony. Most of the songs have Choruses, either in plain or broken time. While Choruses with broken time, naturally and easily arranged, are always popular, yet we cannot resist the impression that plain Choruses where all parts move together are the most effective.

The music is bright and cheerful, and should, as a rule, move off briskly and in strict time, but not too fast. The best effects are often lost by singing a hymn faster than the words can be effectively articulated. Both extremes should be avoided.

The "Orders of Exercises" herein introduced, if persistently used, will give dignity and uniformity to the sessions of the school. The selections of music should be made to suit the lesson for the day, and the index of subjects will be helpful in finding the right hymns. The responses after prayer can be varied, or the same one can be used uniformly in each exercise.

With these suggestions "*Songs of the Golden*" is cordially submitted to our friends of the Sunday School throughout the land.

THE AUTHOR.

SPECIAL NOTICE.—Nearly every piece in this book is copyright property, and all rights to print or reprint its contents, or any part thereof, are reserved exclusively to the proprietor of the same.

ASA HULL'S MUSIC TYPOGRAPHY.

SONGS OF THE GOLDEN.

LIKE A SPARKLING RIVER.

MELIA Z. HAFFNER.   ASA HULL.

1. Life seems but a sparkling riv-er, Flow-ing down the "steep of time,"
2. Cheering pil-grims, faint and wea-ry, And with ten-der-ness and love;
3. We have but a short pro-ba-tion, Soon our la-bors will be o'er;

Bear-ing trust-ing mor-tals ev-er To a ho-ly, hap-py clime.
Pointing thro' earth's darkness drear-y To the glo-rious home a-bove.
Soon from toil and sore temp-ta-tion We shall rest for ev-er-more!

CHORUS.
Let us, then, be up and do-ing, Let us la-bor while we may;
Ros-es round each pathway strewing, Treading soft-ly all the way.

COPYRIGHT, 1896, BY ASA HULL.

THE GOLDEN SHORE.

MARIAN FROELICH.   G. FROELICH.

1. Just a-cross the si-lent riv-er, Where God's hosts a-dore,
2. How the gold-en shore is shin-ing, How it holds the sight!

Spark-ling in a flood of glo-ry Lies the gold-en shore.
Bathed in day that knows no sun-set, Laved in heav-en's light.

REFRAIN.

Oh, the bright, the gold-en shore, Where an-gel-ic hosts a-dore!
Oh, the bright, the bright and golden shore,

Oh, the bright, the gold-en shore, There we'll dwell for ev-er-more.
Oh, the bright, the bright and golden shore,

3 On its banks the songs ne'er languish,
  Endlessly they pour
  To the Lamb their adoration
  On the golden shore.

4 On the golden shore doth beckon
  Till by faith we soar,
  To the flow'r-clad banks of beauty
  On the golden shore.

COPYRIGHT, 1896, BY ASA HULL.

LESSONS OF NATURE.

MARIAN FROELICH. G. FROELICH.

1. The sun sends forth her gold-en beams To gild the but-ter-cup,
2. The hard, un-yield-ing rock, so grey, Gives to the cling-ing vine
3. In God's wise plans the chil-dren hold A place to Him most dear;

The sum-mer cloud sends sil-ver streams That flow'r and leaf may sup;
A help-ing hand, where safe it may Climb where the sun-beams shine;
Then let us be like sun-beams gold, Or na-ture's pass-ing tear,

All na-ture, like its God, doth give To make the earth in beau-ty live;
If we be strong, some weaker one Come let us lift up t'ward God's sun;
For childhood is God's sure de-vice To bring earth nearer Par-a-dise;

All na-ture, like its God, doth give To make the earth in beau-ty live.
If we be strong, some weaker one Come let us lift up t'ward God's sun.
For child-hood is God's sure de-vice To bring earth near-er Par-a-dise.

COPYRIGHT, 1896, BY ASA HULL.

3 Sitting at the feet of Jesus,
  Gladly all His words to hear,
We may drink at wisdom's fountain,
  And our thirsty spirits cheer.

4 Sitting at the feet of Jesus
  Bringeth heaven very nigh,
Fills us with the joy that waiteth
  In His presence, by-and-by.

COPYRIGHT, 1896, BY ASA HULL.

# I WILL PRAISE MY DEAR REDEEMER.

J. E. HALL.   J. E. HALL.

1. I will praise my dear Re-deem-er, I will mag-ni-fy His name;
2. I will praise my dear Re-deem-er With my tongue and with my voice;

I will hon-or and a-dore Him, Who to save from glo-ry came.
Join-ing all the pow'rs with-in me, In His name I will re-joice.

CHORUS.

I will praise my dear Re-deemer, I will mag-ni-fy His name;
  I will praise   His name;

I will praise my dear Re-deem-er, Who to save from glo-ry came.
  I will praise

3 I will praise my dear Redeemer,
  Great His thought, how kind His care;
  O'er my footsteps close He watcheth,
  Loading me with blessings rare.

4 I will praise my dear Redeemer,
  While I tread this earthly soil;
  Praise Him on, and ending never,
  When shall cease this mortal toil.

COPYRIGHT, 1896, BY ASA HULL.

SINGING FOR JESUS.

15

E. RINEHART.   E. RINEHART.

1. Sing-ing for Je-sus all the day long, Sing-ing for Je-sus won-der-ful song;
2. Sing-ing for Je-sus, O what a joy, Sing-ing for Je-sus, bless-ed em-ploy;
3. Sing-ing for Je-sus, Sav-iour di-vine, Sing-ing for Je-sus, Lord, I am Thine;
4. Sing-ing for Je-sus all thro' the night, Sing-ing for Je-sus when it is light;

Trust-ing the full-ness of His love, Jour-ney-ing on to my home a-bove.
Joy of the ran-somed, full and free, O what a bless-ing there comes to me.
O what an o-cean, vast and free, Bound-less His love, for it reach-es me.
Songs of the ran-somed, joy-ful strains, Je-sus, my Sav-iour, for-ev-er reigns.

REFRAIN.

Sing-ing for Je-sus, sing-ing for Je-sus, Sing-ing for Je-sus all the day long;

Sing-ing for Je-sus, bless-ed Re-deem-er, Sing-ing for Je-sus wonderful song!

COPYRIGHT, 1896, BY ASA HULL.

WHEN WE REACH THE GATES OF GOLD—Concluded.

BY COOL SILOAM'S SHADY RILL.

R. HEBER. ASA HULL.

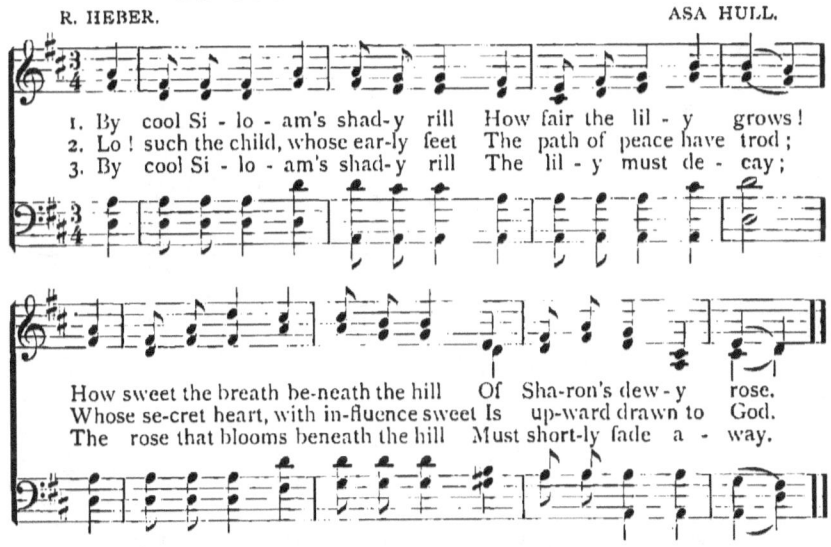

4 And soon, too soon, the wintry hour,
  Of man's maturer age
  Will shake the soul with sorrow's power,
  And stormy passion's rage.

5 Dependent on Thy bounteous breath,
  We seek Thy grace alone,
  In childhood, manhood, age, and death,
  To keep us still Thine own.

COPYRIGHT, 1894, BY ASA HULL.

HIS FOLDED WING.   19

MRS. E. W. CHAPMAN.   JNO. R. BRYANT.

1. I rest beneath the wing Al-might-y, No storm can on me fall;
2. I rest beneath His wing Al-might-y, In calm-ness and re-pose;

His arm of love is un-der-neath me, No dan-ger can ap-pall.
With mer-cy He my cup is crown-ing, My cup with joy o'er-flows.

CHORUS.

Be-neath His fold-ed wing   Is peace and joy di-vine!
    fold-ed wing   joy di-vine!

In qui-et He will keep..... This rest-less soul of mine!
       He will keep   this soul of mine!

3 I rest beneath the wing Almighty,
  It is a covert grand;
  Was ever bliss so sweet, enduring,
  With love on ev'ry hand?

4 I rest beneath the wing Almighty,
  And in its shadow hide;
  Beyond the reach of sin's dominion
  Securely I abide.

COPYRIGHT, 1896, BY ASA HULL.

THE CHRISTIAN SOLDIER.

LANTA WILSON SMITH.   ASA HULL.

Spirited.

1. Stand firm-ly, Chris-tian Sol-dier; A time like this de-mands
2. Stand firm-ly, Chris-tian Sol-dier, Be true in word and deed;
3. Stand firm-ly, Chris-tian Sol-dier, The Cap-tain's word o-bey;

A firm, un-flinch-ing pur-pose, And will-ing heart and hands.
Of men who may be trust-ed, The world has con-stant need.
Fail not when comes the con-flict, Stand no-bly in the fray;

Like val-iant, trust-y war-riors, Stand read-y for the fight,
One false, un-faith-ful sol-dier De-feat on all may bring;
Be firm, and true, and con-stant, With faith and cour-age strong;

Slower.

For foes are all a-bout us Op-po-sing God and right.
True hearts a-lone are wor-thy To bat-tle for our King.
The bat-tle cry is chang-ing To glad, tri-umph-ant song.

COPYRIGHT, 1895, BY ASA HULL.

THE CHRISTIAN SOLDIER—Concluded.

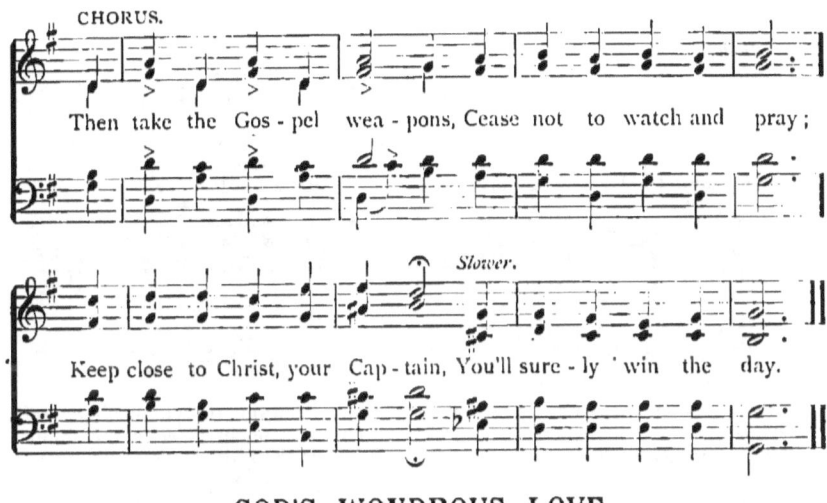

GOD'S WONDROUS LOVE.

MRS. L. M. B. BATEMAN.   ASA HULL.

All sing the melody.

1. Sunshine clear and sunshine bright Fills the earth and sky with light;
2. Soft and sweet the sum-mer air Breathes its fra-grance ev-'ry-where;

So our Sav-iour's wondrous love Fills the earth and sky a-bove!
So God's mer-cy pure and free Lives wher-ev-er mor-tals be.

3 Raindrops fall and falls the dew,
   Ever bounteous, ever new;
   As the river seeks the sea
   God's great kindness floweth free!

4 Notes of gladness, words of praise,
   Let our hearts and voices raise;
   May our love and service be
   His through all eternity.

COPYRIGHT, 1895, BY ASA HULL.

22. HE CALLETH FOR THEE.

Mrs. L. M. BEAL BATEMAN. ASA HULL.

1. Sweet Mary was sitting in sorrow, Who sat at the feet of her Lord;
2. Then Mary arose from her silence, And went her sad way thro' the gloom,
3. She came to His wonderful presence—'Twas blessed indeed to obey—

And Martha, the careful and watchful, Came bringing this comforting word.
The sorrowful, desolate pathway, That led her in grief to the tomb.
She came, with what great satisfaction, To see them the stone roll away.

CHORUS. *A little faster.*

"The Master has come, the Master has come," said she, "And He calleth for thee!...... The Master has come, and He calleth for thee!"........
for thee! for thee!

4 Then out of the silence and darkness,
  Her brother came forth at His word;
  Not waiting, but swiftly obeying,
  Those wonderful words of their Lord.

5 O sinner, in sorrow and silence,
  In dark disappointment and gloom,
  The Master is come, and is calling
  To triumph o'er death and the tomb.

COPYRIGHT, 1896, BY ASA HULL.

FAR OUT ON THE LONELY BILLOW. 23

ROSSITER W. RAYMOND.   FERD. SILCHER. ARR.

1. Far out on the lone-ly bil-low, The sail-or sails the sea,
2. Far down in the earth's dark bo-som, The min-er mines the ore;
A-lone with the night and tem-pest, Where countless dan-gers be.
Death lurks in the dark be-hind him, And in the rock be-fore.

CHORUS.
Yet nev-er a-lone is a Chris-tian, Who lives by faith and prayer;
For God is a Friend un-fail-ing, And God is ev-'ry-where.

3 Forth into the dreadful battle
   The steadfast soldier goes;
   No friend at his hand when dying,
   His eyes to kiss and close.

4 Lord, grant as we sail life's ocean,
   Or delve in mines of woe,
   Or fight in the dreadful conflict,
   This comfort all to know.

COPYRIGHT, 1893, BY D. C. JOHN. *By permission.*

COME UNTO ME—Concluded.

4 Hear, O hear the gracious warning
    Speaking to all !
Comes at evening, noon and morning,
    Hear the call !

Time is flying, swiftly flying,
    Soon no more 'twill be ;
O prepare, prepare for dying,
    "Come unto me !"

26. JESUS KNOWS ALL ABOUT IT.

WM. EDW. PENNEY. ASA HULL.

1. When we are tempted or when we do wrong, Jesus knows all a-bout it;
2. When we are sinful, and when we are sad, Jesus knows all a-bout it;
3. When we to-gether in Sunday school meet, Jesus knows all a-bout it;
4. When we reach up to take hold of His hand, Jesus knows all a-bout it;

When in His cause we are earnest and strong, Jesus knows all a-bout it.
When we o-bey Him, and therefore are glad, Je-sus knows all a-bout it.
When we sing praises, and kneel at His feet, Je-sus knows all a-bout it.
When we set out for the heav-en-ly land, Je-sus knows all a-bout it.

CHORUS.

Yes! He knows all a-bout it, And we will nev-er-more doubt it;

Whatev-er we do, let us keep it in view, That Je-sus knows all a-bout it.

COPYRIGHT, 1896, BY ASA HULL.

TRUSTING IN THE ARK.   29

E. R. LATTA.   CHAS. K. LANGLEY.

1. Tho' heav-y be the clouds and dark, And hid-den be the sun,
2. Tempta-tions thick-ly round may stand, To lead my soul a-stray;

I'm trust-ing in sal-va-tion's ark, And it shall bear me on!
But ev-er t'ward the gold-en strand, My ark shall glide a-way!

CHORUS.

'Tis the ark of love and mer-cy, Sail-ing to the heav'nly shore;
And 'twill safe-ly bear me o-ver, Where my Lord has gone be-fore....

3 Tho' tempests lash the waves to foam,
  No storm shall overwhelm;
  But I shall safely reach my home,
  With Jesus at the helm.

4 My spirit need not feel alarm,
  At all the hosts of sin ;
  My ark will shield my soul from harm,
  If I but stay within.

COPYRIGHT, 1896, BY ASA HULL.

BEACON LIGHTS ARE SHINING.

1. The bil-lows may be roll-ing high, And wild the rag-ing sea,
2. When faith is weak, and hope is faint, Look up a-cross the wave,

But Bea-con Lights are shin-ing bright Up-on the shore for thee.
The Bea-con Lights are shin-ing bright To res-cue and to save.

CHORUS.
O Bea-con Lights, shine on, shine on, The rag-ing bil-lows o'er;
And guide us to the home of love Up-on the fur-ther shore.

3 Look up, O trembling mariner,
   Adrift upon the sea,
For Beacon Lights are shining bright,
   To-night to rescue thee.

4 Have faith in God, and falter not;
   Be trustful and be brave;
The Beacon Lights are shining bright,
   And Christ is strong to save.

COPYRIGHT, 1896, BY ASA HULL.

OH, TO BE SOMETHING—CONCLUDED.

Some - thing, some - thing, Something that's a - ble to bring
Oh, to be something,
Ser - vice, ser - vice To Je - sus, my Sav-iour and King.
Service no mat-ter how hum - ble,

JESUS, SAVIOUR, PILOT ME.

Rev. EDW. HOPPER. J. E. GOULD.

1. Je - sus, Sav - iour, pi - lot me O - ver life's tem-pestuous sea;
D. C. Chart and com-pass come from Thee: Je - sus, Sav - iour, pi - lot me.

Un-known waves be-fore me roll, Hid - ing rock and treach'rous shoal;

2 As a mother stills her child,
  Thou canst hush the ocean wild;
  Boist'rous waves obey Thy will,
  When Thou say'st to them "Be still!"
  Wondrous Sovereign of the sea,
  Jesus, Saviour, pilot me.

3 When at last I near the shore,
  And the fearful breakers roar,
  'Twixt me and the peaceful rest,
  Then, while leaning on Thy breast,
  May I hear Thee say to me,
  "Fear not, I will pilot thee!"

SAVE AND COMFORT ME.

FRANCES V. HUBBARD. FRANK HERMANS.

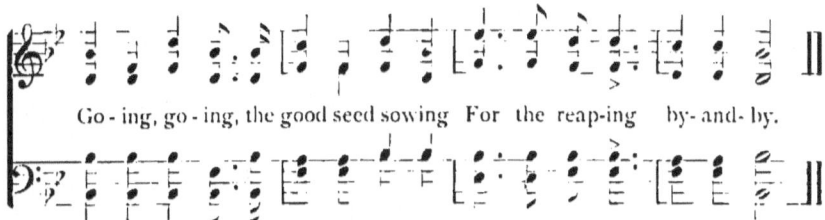

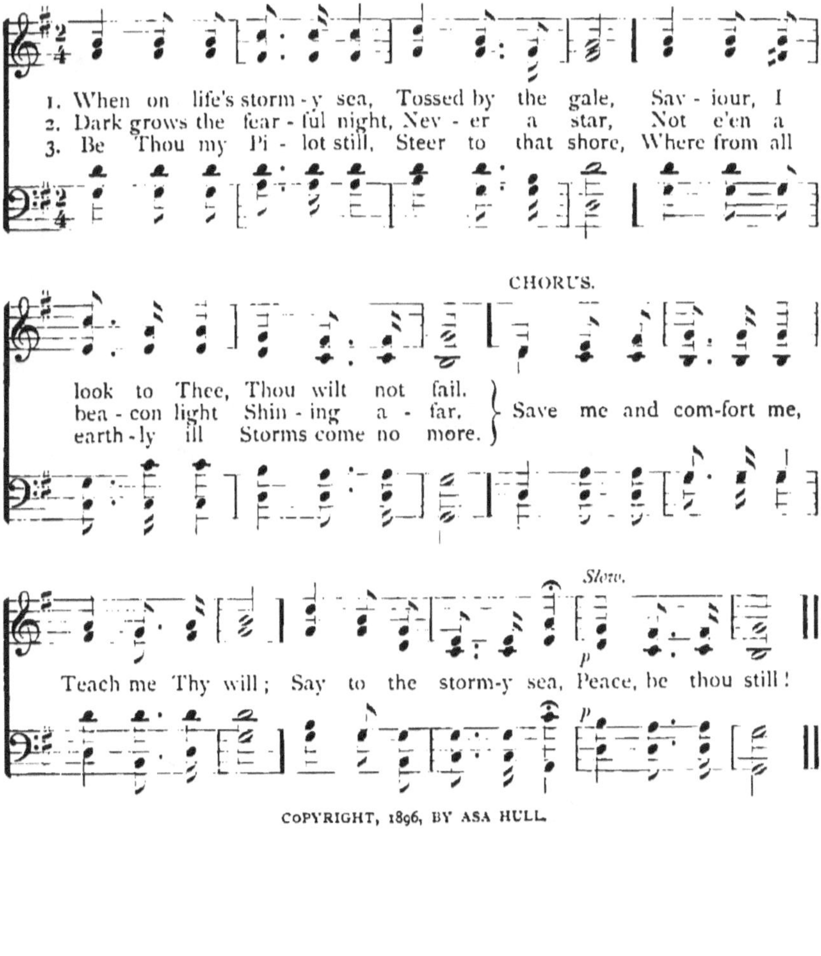

THE TOILERS' SONG—CONCLUDED. 37

ser - vice gives be - low; ...... Sing - ing prais - - - es to
    gives be-low;   prais - es to God, Sing - ing

D. S.

God, ... till we sing the songs the an - gels know;
prais - es to God,

BLEST BE THE TIE.

JOHN FAWCETT.   H. G. NAGELI.

1. Blest be the tie that binds Our hearts in Chris - tian love;
2. Be - fore our Fa - ther's throne We pour our ar - dent prayers;

The fel - low - ship of kin - dred minds Is like to that a - bove.
Our fears, our hopes, our aims are one, Our com - forts and our cares.

3 We share our mutual woes;
   Our mutual burdens bear;
   And often for each other flows
     The sympathizing tear.

4 When we asunder part,
   It gives us inward pain;
   But we shall still be joined in heart,
     And hope to meet again.

BLESSED MASTER, SEND ME.

39

CHAS. H. GABRIEL. CHAS. H. GABRIEL.

1. There's a might-y work to do, And the Mas-ter calls for you;
2. In the fields of rip-ened grain, There is work the fruits to gain;
3. Let us, then, with sweet ac-cord, All be read-y for the Lord,

Let each heart's glad an-swer be, "Bless-ed Mas-ter, oh, send me."
Let the cry be full and free, "Bless-ed Mas-ter, oh, send me."
And with this our strong-est plea, "Bless-ed Mas-ter, oh, send me."

CHORUS.

Work of mer-cy, work of love, Work of Him who reigns a-bove,
Guid-ed by a lov-ing hand, Let us work at God's com-mand.

COPYRIGHT, 1896, BY ASA HULL.

40 THE LIGHT OF LOVE.

IDA L. REED. ASA HULL.

1. Fill my days, dear Lord, with light, Long my faith hath shad-owed been;
2. Fill my heart, dear Lord, with light, Lift the shad-ows, oh, I pray!
3. Pa - tient - ly, dear Lord, a - lone I have passed through sor-row's night;

From my heart dis - pel the night, Let the light of love shine in.
Let Thy love shine warm and bright, All a - long the dark - some way.
Wea - ri - ly the hours have flown, Fill my soul at last with light.

D.S. From my heart dis - pel the night, Let the light of love shine in.

CHORUS. D. S.

Shine in, shine in, Let the light of love shine in;....
Shine in, shine in,

WONDERFUL RICHES.

REV. JOHN O. FOSTER. CHAS. K. LANGLEY.

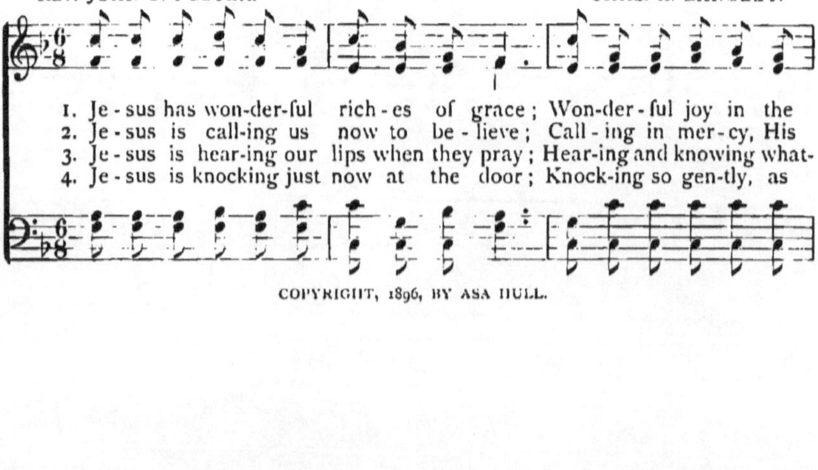

1. Je - sus has won-der-ful rich - es of grace; Won-der-ful joy in the
2. Je - sus is call-ing us now to be - lieve; Call - ing in mer - cy, His
3. Je - sus is hear-ing our lips when they pray; Hear-ing and knowing what-
4. Je - sus is knocking just now at the door; Knock-ing so gen-tly, as

COPYRIGHT, 1896, BY ASA HULL.

SCATTER SUNSHINE AND GLADNESS—Concluded. 43

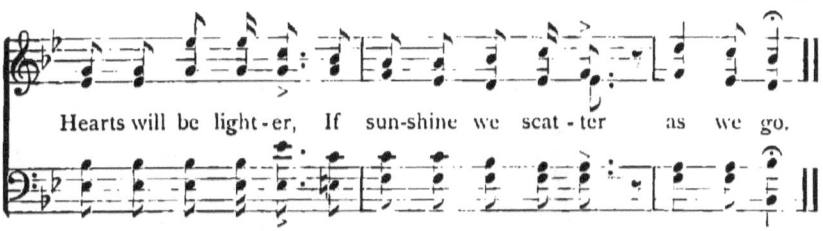

Hearts will be light-er, If sun-shine we scat-ter as we go.

FORGET ME NOT.

WM. EDW. PENNEY. ASA HULL.

1. "For-get me not,"........ we oft-en say,....... When friend from
    "For-get me not,"   we oft-en say,
friend.... is torn a-way;..... Forget me not...... when ocean
When friend from friend   is torn a-way;   Forget me not

Ral - len - tan - do.

wide....... Between us rolls....... its might-y tide.........
when ocean wide   Between us rolls its might-y tide, its mighty tide.

2 " Forget me not," our sad hearts cry,
  While weary years of waiting fly ;
  Forget me not, we sigh at last,
  When life's short day for us is past.

3 " Forget me not," the Christian cries,
  His face upturned toward the skies ;
  O Father, whatsoe'er my lot,
  In life, in death, forget me not.

COPYRIGHT, 1894, BY ASA HULL.

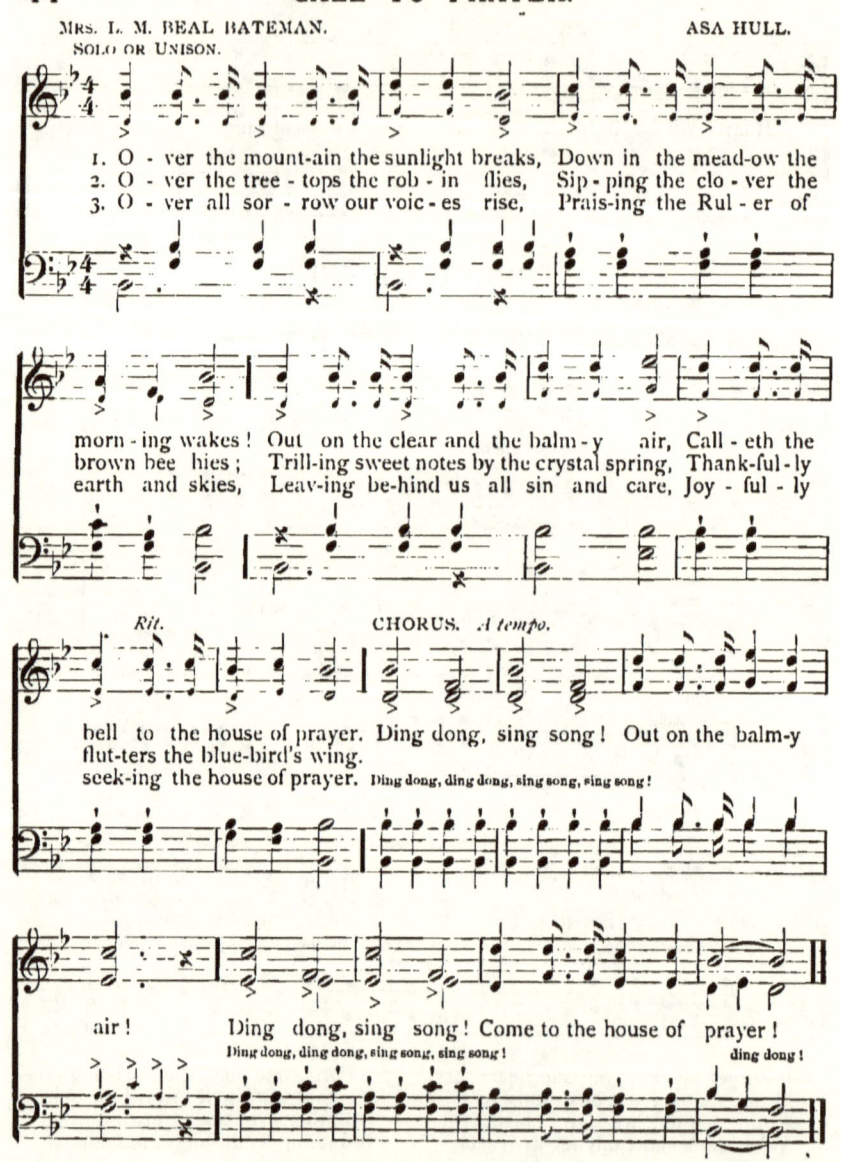

SWEET ZION BELLS.

45

Mrs. A. L. DAVISON. J. H. FILLMORE.

1. { O'er heav'n-ly plains the gold-en chimes Of Zi-on ring to-day;
   { For pass-ing souls those chimes are rung, To [OMIT............]
   guide them on their way.

REFRAIN.
Sweet chimes of Zi-on bells, Sweet chim-ing Zi-on bells,
Sweet bells,............................Sweet bells,...
They cheer us on our pleas-ant way;
sweet bells, They cheer our way,..........
Sweet chiming bells, They cheer us on our pleasant way, Sweet chiming bells.
They cheer our way,........

2 And we, who walk in earthly vales,
  Their joyful music hear,
  In melody divinely sweet,
  So faint and yet so clear.

3 They call us home, not here our rest,
  They softly seem to say;
  Beyond the gates of Zion fair
  There shines a brighter day.

COPYRIGHT, 1882, BY FILLMORE BROS. BY PER.

JESUS CALLS FOR WORKERS—Concluded. 47

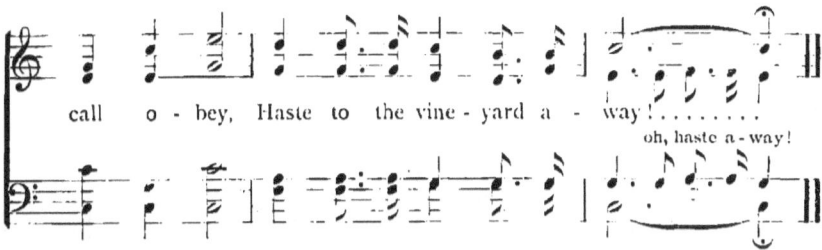

call o-bey, Haste to the vine-yard a-way!........
oh, haste a-way!

THE HILLS OF AMETHYST.

MRS. P. J. OWENS.   HARRY SANDERS.

Moderato.

1. Lift thine eyes un-to the hills, Thou in sadness weeping; There a joy-ous
2. Dost thou miss the golden grain, Snowy buds immortal? Would'st thou have them

CHORUS.

mur-mur thrills, From the an-gels reap-ing. Death is but the morning mist,
back a-gain? Look at heav-en's por-tal.

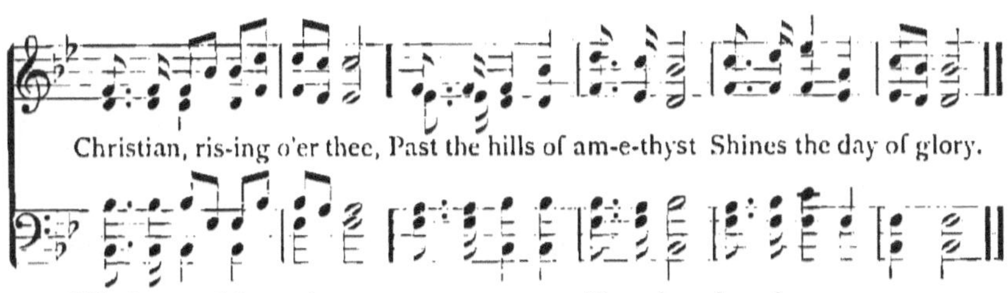

Christian, ris-ing o'er thee, Past the hills of am-e-thyst Shines the day of glory.

3 Lift thy tearful eyes in trust,
   Christ, thy treasures keeping,
   He who measures earthly dust,
   Human tear-drops weeping.

4 Dost thou fear the open grave,
   Fear death's narrow prison?
   Jesus died the lost to save,
   Jesus hath arisen.

COPYRIGHT, 1871, BY ASA HULL.

BEYOND THE SHADOWS

ANNIE HERBERT. ASA HULL.

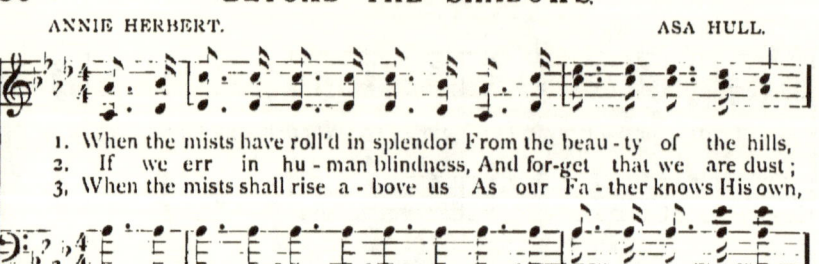

1. When the mists have roll'd in splendor From the beau-ty of the hills,
2. If we err in hu-man blindness, And for-get that we are dust;
3. When the mists shall rise a-bove us As our Fa-ther knows His own,

And the sunshine warm and ten-der Falls in kiss-es on the rills,
If we miss the law of kindness, When we strug-gle to be just:
Face to face with those that love us, We shall know as we are known.

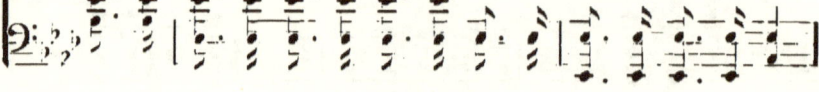

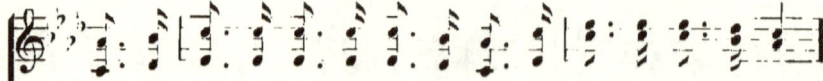

We may read love's shining let-ter In the rain-bow of the spray:
Snow-y wings of peace shall cov-er All the pain that clouds our day,
Just be-yond the darken'd shadows Floats the gold-en fringe of day;

We shall know each oth-er bet-ter, When the mists have clear'd a-way.
When the wea-ry watch is o-ver, And the mists have clear'd a-way.
We shall see its wondrous brightness, When the mists have clear'd a-way.

COPYRIGHT, 1896, BY ASA HULL.

BEYOND THE SHADOWS—Concluded.

JESUS, REFUGE OF MY SOUL.

C. WESLEY. *Music on page 179.*

1 JESUS, refuge of my soul,
   Let me to Thy bosom fly,
 While the nearer waters roll,
   While the tempest still is high;
 Hide me, O my Saviour, hide,
   Till the storm of life is past;
 Safe into the haven guide,
   O receive my soul at last.

2 Other refuge have I none;
   Hangs my helpless soul on Thee:
 Leave, O leave me not alone;
   Still support and comfort me:
 All my trust on Thee is stay'd;
   All my help from Thee I bring;
 Cover my defenceless head
   With the shadow of Thy wing.

3 Thou, O Christ, art all I want:
   More than all in Thee I find:
 Raise the fallen, cheer the faint,
   Heal the sick, and lead the blind,
 Just and holy is Thy name;
   I am all unrighteousness;
 False, and full of sin I am;
   Thou art full of truth and grace.

4 Plenteous grace with Thee is found,
   Grace to cover all my sin:
 Let the healing streams abound;
   Make and keep me pure within.
 Thou of life the fountain art;
   Freely let me take of Thee:
 Spring Thou up within my heart;
   Rise to all eternity.

WHITER THAN SNOW.—CONCLUDED. 53

OUR OFFERING BRING.

W. B. CARNES.
INFANT CLASS.
J. H. ROSECRANS.

1. A happy band of children, We're battling for our King; With willing hearts we
2. We bring no cost-ly treasure To lay at Jesus' feet; But yet it gives us

CHORUS. BY THE SCHOOL.

serve Him, And each our off'ring bring. Oh, hap-py band of chil-dren, Now
pleas-ure The sto-ry to re-peat.

battling for your King; With willing hearts to serve Him, Let each your off'ring bring.

3 Then take our humble off'ring—
  It is the children's mite;
  We know the Saviour tells us,
  "'Tis precious in His sight."

4 We'll send the blessed story
  To those in heathen lands;
  To tell them of His glory,
  We'll lend our hearts and hands.

COPYRIGHT, 1893, BY ASA HULL.

AT THE SETTING OF THE SUN—Concluded.

com-ing, To reck-on with His servants at the set-ting of the sun;
It may not be your mis-sion, it will not be my du-ty, To
tell Him of the la-bors that oth-ers may have done.

4 Then let us still be faithful, though oft our steps be weary,
Nor look behind and loiter, or sigh o'er tasks undone,
But press with vigor onward, all doubtings overcoming,
That He may well reward us at setting of the sun.

WHAT A FRIEND WE HAVE IN JESUS.

1 What a friend we have in Jesus,
All our sins and griefs to bear;
What a privilege to carry
Everything to Him in prayer.
O, what peace we often forfeit,
O, what needless pain we bear;
All because we do not carry
Everything to Him in prayer.

2 Have we trials and temptations?
Is there trouble anywhere?
We should never be discouraged,
Take it to the Lord in prayer.

Can we find a friend so faithful,
Who will all our sorrows share?
Jesus knows our ev'ry weakness,
Take it to the Lord in prayer.

3 Are we weak and heavy-laden,
Cumbered with a load of care,
Precious Saviour, still our refuge,
Take it to the Lord in prayer.
Do thy friends despise, forsake thee,
Take it to the Lord in prayer;
In His arms He'll take and shield thee,
Thou wilt find a solace there.

Dr. H. Bonar.

SOWING SEEDS OF GOOD OR ILL—Concluded.

Sow - ing, sow - ing, Count-less seeds of good or ill;
We are sow - ing, dai - ly sow - ing,
Sow - ing, sow - ing, On rich soil or bar - ren hill.
Sow-ing on the fer - tile low - lands,

CHRIST OUR FRIEND.

Rev. Thos. L. Poulson. J. G. Robinson.

1. Tho' the night o'erhang our dwell-ing, And the tem-pests round us rave;
2. Still the gos-pel stream-lets flow-ing To the hearts of all man-kind,
And the win-try blasts are swell-ing, Till we fear there's none to save:
And the heav'n-ly breez-es blow-ing, Cheer the wait-ing, trust-ing mind.

3 With the Christian's ban-ner o'er us,
  As to duty we attend ;
  In the wide world spread before us
  Christ shall ever be our friend.

4 In the morning of His coming,
  When the warfare all is past,
  We'll be counted in the morning
  Of His jewels at the last.

60. FROM O'ER THE SEA.

E. RINEHART. ASA HULL.
DUET.*

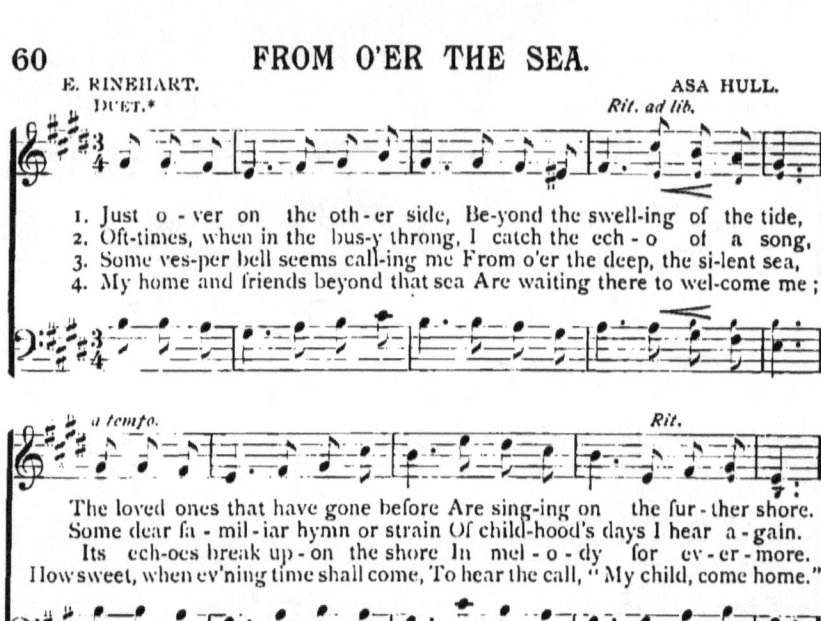

1. Just o-ver on the oth-er side, Be-yond the swell-ing of the tide,
2. Oft-times, when in the bus-y throng, I catch the ech-o of a song,
3. Some ves-per bell seems call-ing me From o'er the deep, the si-lent sea,
4. My home and friends beyond that sea Are waiting there to wel-come me;

The loved ones that have gone before Are sing-ing on the fur-ther shore.
Some dear fa-mil-iar hymn or strain Of child-hood's days I hear a-gain.
Its ech-oes break up-on the shore In mel-o-dy for ev-er-more.
How sweet, when ev'ning time shall come, To hear the call, "My child, come home."

CHORUS. *A little faster.*

From o'er the sea,........ the crys-tal sea,........ There comes a
From o'er the sea, the crys-tal sea,

strange,... sweet mel-o-dy;...... And from the land..... beyond that
There comes a strange, sweet mel-o-dy; And from the land

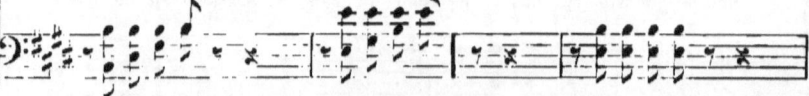

* A single voice on each part, or all the Sopranos and Altos can sing the upper part—Tenors and Basses sing the lower part.

COPYRIGHT, 1896, BY ASA HULL.

FROM O'ER THE SEA—CONCLUDED.

JESUS LOVES LITTLE CHILDREN.

Mrs. JENNIE ZEH. CHAS. L. MOORE.

1. Je - sus loves you, lit - tle chil-dren, If you'll close be-side Him stay;
2. Je - sus is the friend of chil-dren, And He wants you for His friend;
3. Je - sus calls for lit - tle chil-dren, Great and glo-rious King is He!

He will feed you, from harm keep you, Smooth and pleasant make the way.
If you'll on - ly trust Him, children, He'll be faith - ful to the end.
Yet He says of lit - tle children, "Suf-fer them to come to Me."

D. S. 'Tis the Sav-iour who is call - ing, Will you heed His words to-day?

CHORUS.   D. S

"Suf - fer, suf - fer lit - tle chil-dren, Suf-fer them to come to me;"

COPYRIGHT, 1893, BY ASA HULL.

THE ARMOR OF GOD.--CONCLUDED.

O, THINK OF A HOME OVER THERE.

1 O, THINK of a home over there,
    By the side of the river of light,
    Where the saints, all immortal and fair,
    Are robed in their garments of white.
    ‖: Over there, over there, over there,
        O, think of a home over there. :‖

2 O, think of the friends over there,
    Who before us the journey have trod,
    Of the songs that they breathe on the air,
    In their home in the palace of God.
    ‖: Over there, over there, over there,
        O, think of the friends over there. :‖

3 My Saviour is now over there;   [rest:
    There my kindred and friends are at
    Then away from my sorrow and care,
    Let me fly to the land of the blest.
    ‖: Over there, over there, over there,
        My Saviour is now over there. :‖

4 I'll soon be at home over there,
    For the end of my journey I see;
    Many dear to my heart, over there,
    Are watching and waiting for me.
    ‖: Over there, over there, over there,
        I'll soon be at home over there. :‖

64. CHOOSE YE, ONE AND ALL.

Mrs. L. M. Beal Bateman. — Asa Hull.

1. On-ly one moment at once goes by, Swift-ly, tho' one at a time they fly;
2. On-ly one step at a time we take, As on life's journey our way we make;

Lad-en by mor-tals as mortals will, Bearing their bur-dens of good or ill.
One step to glo-ry or one to woe, Ours is the choice of which path we go.

CHORUS.
Choose of the tri-fles for one and all, Mountains are made of the at-oms small;
Live at your best as the moments fly, Worth will be wealth as the years roll by.

3 Only one thing can our frail hands do,
As we the labors of life pursue;
Labors of loving or works of hate,
Make the world joyful or desolate.

4 Only one thought at a time the brain
Carries of wisdom or folly vain;
Food for the spirit, or poisoned taste,
Going to growing or gone to waste.

COPYRIGHT, 1896, BY ASA HULL.

3 Follow the flag of Jesus,
   Satan's intrenchments break;
   Where it is borne before you,
   Follow for Jesus' sake.

4 Follow the flag of Jesus,
   Ever, through good and ill;
   Knowing, where'er it leadeth,
   He will be with you still.

EVER PRESS ONWARD.

75

E. R. LATTA.
JNO. R. BRYANT.

1. Ev-er press onward, ye pilgrim band, Seeking a coun-try ev-er fair;
2. Ev-er press onward, in spite of ills That may be-fore you thick-ly rise;

Ev-er press onward where Je-sus leads, If you would dwell with Him there.
Ev-er press onward, by faith to view Where the blest Ca-na-an lies.

CHORUS.

Ever press onward with gladsome song, Onward till faith is lost in sight;

Rit.

Ev-er press onward, a youthful throng—On to heav'n's por-tals so bright.

3 Ever press onward, though foes ye meet,
Trusting that ye shall overcome;
Ever press onward, whate'er would cheat
You of that beautiful home.

4 Ever press onward, in joy and hope,
Tow'rd a land that's free from sin;
Ever press onward, till life shall end,
End with the entering in.

COPYRIGHT, 1896, BY ASA HULL.

WHERE THE GATES ARE OPEN—Concluded.

COMING TO THE CROSS.

Rev. Wm. McDonald. Wm. G. Fischer.

1. I am coming to the cross;
   I am poor, and weak, and blind;
   I am counting all but dross;
   I shall full salvation find.

Cho.—I am trusting, Lord, in Thee,
   Dear Lamb of Calvary;
   Humbly at Thy cross I bow;
   Save me, Jesus, save me now.

2 Long my heart has sighed for Thee;
  Long has evil reigned within;
  Jesus sweetly speaks to me,
  I will cleanse you from all sin.

3 Here I give my all to Thee,—
  Friends, and time, and earthly store;
  Soul and body Thine to be—
  Wholly Thine—for evermore.

4 In the promises I trust;
  Now I feel the blood applied;
  I am prostrate in the dust;
  I with Christ am crucified.

5 Jesus comes! He fills my soul!
  Perfected in love I am;
  I am every whit made whole;
  Glory, glory to the Lamb.

EVENTIDE.
REV. H. LYTE. W. H. MONK.

1. Abide with me! Fast falls the eventide; The darkness deepens; Lord, with me abide!
2. Not a brief glance I beg, a parting word; But as Thou dwell'st with Thy disciples, Lord,

When other helpers fail and comforts flee, Help of the helpless, O abide with me!
Familiar, condescending, patient, free, Come not to sojourn, but abide with me!

3 I need Thy presence ev'ry passing hour;
What but Thy grace can foil the tempter's power?
Who like Thyself my guide and stay can be?
Through cloud and sunshine, O abide with me!

4 Hold Thou Thy cross before my closing eyes;
Shine through the gloom, and point me to the skies;
Heav'n's morning breaks, and earth's vain shadows flee;
In life, in death, O Lord, abide with me.

3 Tell that I'm coming to Jesus,
    Seeking salvation;
  Many will scoff at His offer—
    But will not I.

4 Tell that I'm coming to Jesus,
    Trusting His promise;
  He will perform it, nor leave me
    Hopeless to die.

BOUGHT WITH A PRICE—CONCLUDED.

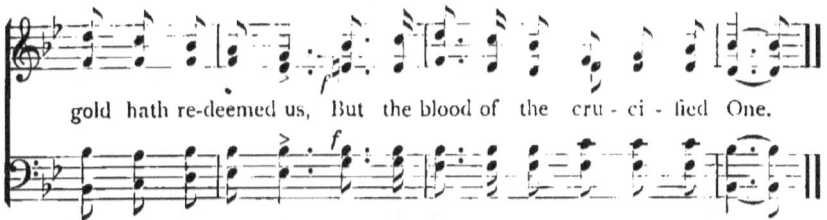

gold hath re-deemed us, But the blood of the cru - ci - fied One.

4 Then the Lord will abundantly pardon,
And your sins be remembered no more,
While your heart will o'erflow with thanksgiving
For unspeakable blessings in store.

DEAR LORD, REMEMBER ME.

ISAAC WATTS.   Music and Chorus by ASA HULL.

1. A - las! and did my Sav - iour bleed? And did my Sov -'reign die?
CHO. { Help me dear Sav-iour, Thee to own, And ev - er faith-ful be;
       { Re - mem - ber me, re - mem - ber me, Dear Lord, re - mem - ber me;

Would He de - vote that sa - cred head For such a worm as I?
And when Thou sit - test on Thy throne, Dear Lord, re - mem - ber me.
And when Thou sit - est, etc. (2d part of chorus can be sung or omitted ad. lib.)

2 Was it for crimes that I have done
   He groaned upon the tree?
   Amazing pity! grace unknown!
   And love beyond degree.

3 Well might the sun in darkness hide,
   And shut his glory in,
   When Christ, the mighty Maker, died
   For man, the creature's, sin.

4 Thus might I hide my blushing face
   While His dear cross appears;
   Dissolve my heart in thankfulness,
   And melt mine eyes to tears.

5 But drops of grief can ne'er repay
   The debt of love I owe;
   Here, Lord, I give myself away,—
   'Tis all that I can do.

COPYRIGHT, 1867, BY ASA HULL. RE-ENTERED, 1896.

ROLL AWAY THE STONE.

1. Gath-er'd round the grave of Laz-'rus, Friends and two fond sisters weep;
'Tis the loss of friend and broth-er, Fills their hearts with anguish deep.

2. See! the Son of God is pray-ing, See Him there in sor-row bow;
See, oh, see! how much He loved him Who lies cold and si-lent now.

CHORUS.
Come, and roll a-way the stone, Come, and roll a-way the stone;
Let no hin-drance bar the way, Come, and roll a-way the stone.

3 Friends and mourners, cease your weep-
Ye shall see the dead revive; [ing,
Jesus speaks the word of power,
And the dead comes forth alive.
CHO. They have rolled away the stone,
They have rolled away the stone;
Now no hindrance bars the way,
They have rolled away the stone.

4 See! his hands and feet are fasten'd,
Fasten'd so he cannot walk;
While his face is bound with grave-
He can neither see nor talk. [clothes,
CHO. Loose him now and let him go,
Loose him now and let him go;
Let no hindrance bar the way;
Loose him now and let him go.

COPYRIGHT, 1888, BY ASA HULL.

SAVIOUR, REFUGE. 91

A. A. HOYT.   REV. E. A. HOFFMAN.

1. Sav-iour, ref - uge, Son of God, Take me to Thy shelt'ring fold;
2. Thou the an - ti - dote for sin; Thou the fount-ain, pure and good;
3. Tho' I walk the shadowy vale Of temp - ta - tion, pain and care,

Hide me from life's stormy flood, Keep me in Thy rock-bound hold.
Wash my heart, and keep me clean In Thine all - a - ton - ing blood.
Thou wilt all my sor-rows heal— I no e - vil then can fear.

CHORUS.

Sav-iour mine, Lord, di - vine, Ver-y help - less I come;
Sav-iour, Saviour mine, Lord of life di-vine, Ver-y helpless, Lord, now to Thee I come;

Save Thy weak, de-fenceless child, Bring me to Thy kingdom home.

4 O Thou matchless Son of Grace,
  Thou art all I want or know;
  Let Thy streams of heavenly peace,
  To my thirsty spirit flow.

5 Thou, the life from death and tomb,
  Hide me, O my Lord, in Thee;
  When Thou, Christ, my life shalt come,
  Let me then Thy glory see.

COPYRIGHT, 1894, BY THE HOFFMAN MUSIC CO. *By permission.*

THERE'S ROOM AT THE FEAST—Concluded. 93

REFRAIN.

Oh, come from the North and the South, And come from the West and the East;
Oh, why will you hun-ger and thirst? There's plen-ty of room at the feast.

OLIVET.

RAY PALMER. L. MASON.

1. My faith looks up to Thee, Thou Lamb of Cal-va-ry, Sav-iour Di-vine!
2. May Thy rich grace impart Strength to my fainting heart, My zeal in-spire!

{ Now hear me while I pray; } O, let me, from this day, Be whol-ly Thine!
{ Take all my guilt a-way;   }
{ As Thou hast died for me, } Pure, warm and changeless be—A liv-ing fire!
{ O, may my love to Thee   }

3 While life's dark maze I tread,
  And griefs around me spread,
    Be Thou my guide;
  Bid darkness turn to day,
  Wipe sorrow's tears away,
  Nor let me ever stray
    From Thee aside.

4 When ends life's transient dream,
  When death's cold sullen stream
    Shall o'er me roll,
  Blest Saviour! then, in love,
  Fear and distrust remove;
  O, bear me safe above—
    A ransomed soul!

SAIL NOT WITHOUT THE MASTER—Concluded.

THE TEMPERANCE BANNER.
(For the foregoing Music.)

1 Unfurl the temp'rance banner,
 And let it proudly wave;
 Let sons and daughters gather
 Fair freedom's land to save.
 From mountain, hill and valley
 Let teeming millions come!
 And round the banner rally,
 Defenders of our home!
 CHO. Then raise the temp'rance banner,
  And let it proudly wave;
  ‖: Let sons and daughters gather
   Fair freedom's land to save! :‖

2 Unfurl the temp'rance banner,
 And let the strong and brave
 Renew the glorious conflict,
 The fallen seek to save;
 And rouse, ye men of valor,
 Be steadfast, firm and true,
 Though long and fierce the battle,
 The vict'ry is for you!
 CHO. Then raise the temp'rance banner,
  And let it proudly wave;
  ‖: Let sons and daughters gather
   Fair freedom's land to save! :‖

Rev. M. L. Hofford.

GIVE ME THE WORLD FOR JESUS—Concluded.

earn-est, my heartfelt pe-ti-tion, That I may bring it to Cal-va-ry's cross.

CORONATION.

Rev. Edw. Perronet. Oliver Holden.

1. All hail the power of Je-sus' name! Let an-gels pros-trate fall;
2. Ye cho-sen seed of Is-rael's race, Ye ran-somed from the fall,
3. Sin-ners, whose love can ne'er for-get The wormwood and the gall,

Bring forth the roy-al di-a-dem, And crown Him Lord of all!
Hail Him who saves you by His grace, And crown Him Lord of all!
Go, spread your trophies at His feet, And crown Him Lord of all!

Bring forth the roy-al di-a-dem, And crown Him Lord of all!
Hail Him who saves you by His grace, And crown Him Lord of all!
Go, spread your trophies at His feet, And crown Him Lord of all!

4 Let every kindred, every tribe,
On this terrestrial ball,
To Him all majesty ascribe,
And crown Him Lord of all!

5 Oh, that with yonder sacred throng,
We at His feet may fall!
We'll join the everlasting song,
And crown Him Lord of all!

REJOICE AND BE GLAD! 99

HORATIUS BONAR.   D. C. JOHN.

1. Re - joice and be glad! the Re - deem-er has come! Go, look on His cra-dle, His cross, and His tomb. Rejoice and be glad! it is sunshine at last; The clouds have departed, the shadows have past. Re-joice, ... Rejoice, ... for the Lamb that was slain, O'er death is triumphant, and liveth again.
2. Re - joice and be glad! for the blood hath been shed; Re-demption is fin-ish'd, the price hath been paid. Rejoice and be glad! now the pardon is free; The Just for the un-just has died on the tree.
3. Re - joice and be glad! for our King is on high, He plead-eth for us on His throne in the sky. Rejoice and be glad! for He cometh a-gain, He com-eth in glo - ry, the Lamb that was slain. Rejoice and be glad! Rejoice and be glad!

COPYRIGHT, 1893, BY D. C. JOHN. *By permission.*

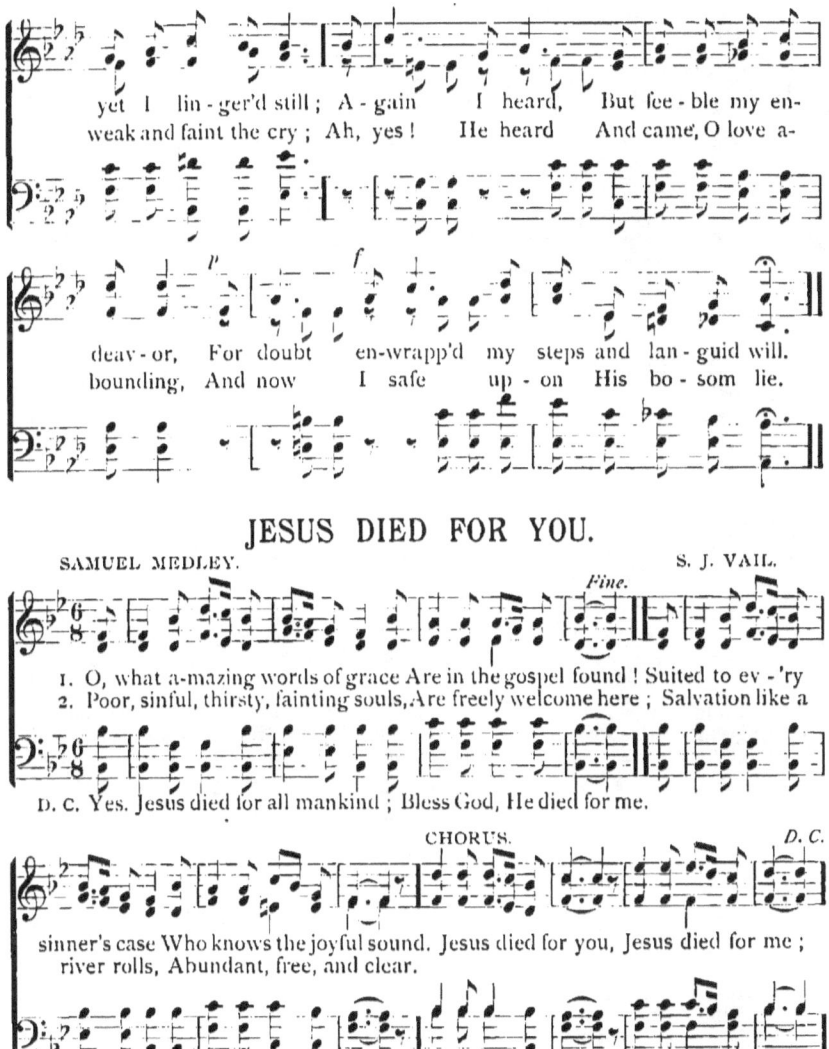

NO BOOK IS LIKE THE BIBLE.

FANNY J. CROSBY.   ASA HULL.

3 Oh, let us love the Bible,
  And praise it more and more;
  Our life is like a shadow,
  Our days will soon be o'er;
  But if we closely follow
  The counsel God has given,
  We then may hope with angels
  To sing His praise in heaven.

COPYRIGHT, 1869 AND 1879, BY ASA HULL.

SOMETHING EVERY DAY—Concluded.

Fa-ther watch-es o-ver you. Oh! you can-not reck-on till e-ter-ni-ty, What the bless-ed har-vest is to be.

JESUS IS MINE.

ARRANGED.

Adagio e legato.

1. { Fade, fade, each earthly joy, Je - sus is mine! }
   { Break ev-'ry ten-der tie, Je - sus is mine! }
   Dark is the wil-der-ness; Earth has no rest-ing place; Je-sus a-lone can bless; Je-sus is mine!

2 Tempt not my soul away;
  Jesus is mine!
  Here would I ever stay;
  Jesus is mine!
  Perishing things of clay,
  Born but for one brief day,
  Pass from my heart away;
  Jesus is mine!

3 Farewell, ye dreams of night,
  Jesus is mine!
  Lost in this dawning bright,
  Jesus is mine!
  All that my soul has tried
  Left but a dismal void;
  Jesus has satisfied;
  Jesus is mine!

THE HARBOR LIGHT.

E. RINEHART. ASA HULL.

1. The sea runs deep, the night is dark, And dangers crowd my fragile bark,
2. When on life's boundless sea we're toss'd, Our fears prevail and all seems lost,
When o'er the wa-ters clear and bright There flashes out the har-bor light.
When stars are dim, and black the night, Then bright-ly gleams the harbor light.

CHORUS.
Oh! har-bor light, blest har-bor light, Shine on, shine on thro' life's dark night;
O'er trackless seas and rocks and shoals, A lamp and guide to heav'n-bound souls.

3 Blest harbor light, that marks the way
   Into the broad and quiet bay,
   Where storm-tossed souls shall ever rest
   Upon its shore among the blest.

4 Shine on through ages yet to be,
   Oh! harbor light on Calvary,
   And let thy beams illume the way
   From earth to God's eternal day.

COPYRIGHT, 1888 and 1896, BY ASA HULL.

THE SABBATH SCHOOL—Concluded.   109

THE BORDER LINE.

E. R. LATTA.   CHAS. EDW. POLLOCK.

1. Oh, the beau-ties we shall see, When we reach the land di-vine!
2. There, 'tis day, with-out the sun, For the face of God doth shine;

We shall know the mys-ter-y When we cross the bor-der line.
And the night shall ne'er come on, When we cross the bor-der line.

D.S. With a glad-ness of the heart Shall we cross the bor-der line?

CHORUS.

When we're bid-den to de-part, Shall we know the coun-ter-sign?

3 There, we shall no burden bear,
  And our hearts shall ne'er repine;
  We shall never know a care,
  When we cross the border line.

4 Help us Lord, to pray the prayer,
  "Not my will be done, but Thine!"
  We will praise Thee, over there,
  When we cross the border line.

COPYRIGHT, 1896, BY ASA HULL.

THE ARK OF SALVATION—Concluded.

A song of thanksgiving to Christ on the way, For He is the "Mighty to save.!"

JERUSALEM, THE GOLDEN.

J. M. NEALE.   REV. H. L. JENNER.

1. Je-ru-sa-lem the golden! With milk and honey blest; Beneath thy contem-
2. They stand, those halls of Zion, All jubilant with song, And bright with many an
3. O sweet and blessed country, The home of God's elect! O sweet and blessed

pla-tion Sink heart and voice opprest. I know not, O! I know not What
an-gel, And all the mar-tyr throng. There is the throne of Da-vid, And
coun-try, That ea-ger hearts ex-pect! Je-sus, in mer-cy bring us To

joys a-wait me there; What ra-diancy of glo-ry, What bliss beyond compare.
there from toil released, The shout of them that triumph, The song of them that feast.
that dear land of rest; Who art with God the Father And Spirit, ev-er blest.

FAIR GALILEE—Concluded.

JUST AS I AM.

CHARLOTTE ELLIOTT. WM. B. BRADBURY.

1. Just as I am, with-out one plea, But that Thy blood was shed for me,
2. Just as I am, and wait-ing not To rid my soul of one dark blot,

And that Thou bidst me come to Thee, O Lamb of God, I come, I come.
To Thee, whose blood can cleanse each spot, O Lamb of God, I come, I come.

3 Just as I am, poor, wretched, blind,
  Sight, riches, healing of the mind,
  Yea, all I need in Thee I find;
    O Lamb of God, I come, I come.

4 Just as I am, though toss'd about,
  With many a conflict, many a doubt,
  Fightings within, and fears without,—
    O Lamb of God, I come, I come.

5 Just as I am, Thou wilt receive,
  Wilt welcome, pardon, cleanse, relieve;
  Because Thy promise I believe,
    O Lamb of God, I come, I come.

6 Just as I am, Thy love unknown
  Hath broken every barrier down;
  Now to be Thine, yea, Thine alone,
    O Lamb of God, I come, I come.

THE HANDWRITING ON THE WALL—Concluded.

WORK, FOR THE NIGHT IS COMING.

1. Work, for the night is coming,
   Work through the morning hours,
   Work while the dew is sparkling,
   Work 'mid springing flow'rs;
   Work, when the day grows brighter,
   Work in the glowing sun;
   Work, for the night is coming,
   When man's work is done.

2. Work, for the night is coming,
   Work through the sunny noon;
   Fill brightest hours with labor,—
   Rest comes sure and soon:
   Give ev'ry flying minute
   Something to keep in store;
   Work, for the night is coming,
   When man works no more.

3. Work, for the night is coming,
   Under the sunset skies;
   While their bright tints are glowing,
   Work, for the daylight flies;
   Work, till the last beam fadeth,
   Fadeth to shine no more;
   Work, while the night is dark'ning,
   When man's work is o'er.

4. Work, for the night is coming,
   Work, while the fields are white;
   Work, for thy sands are running,
   Work, while hopes are bright;
   Gather thy sheaves of morning;
   Rest not thy hand at noon;
   Labor and strive till evening;
   Rest when daylight's gone.

Sidney Dyer.

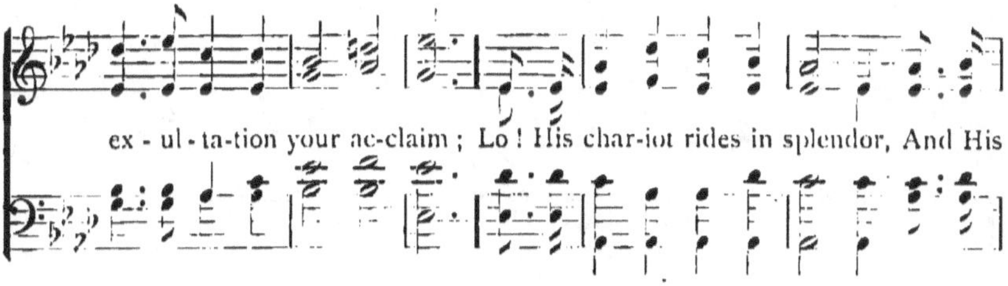

THE KING'S ADVANCE—CONCLUDED.

Strike, strike, strike the cymbal, Strike, strike, strike a-gain, Shout a-loud with ex-ul-ta-tion your ac-claim; Lo! His char-iot rides in splendor, And His roy-al train Songs of tri-umph loud-ly ren-der, In a might-y strain!

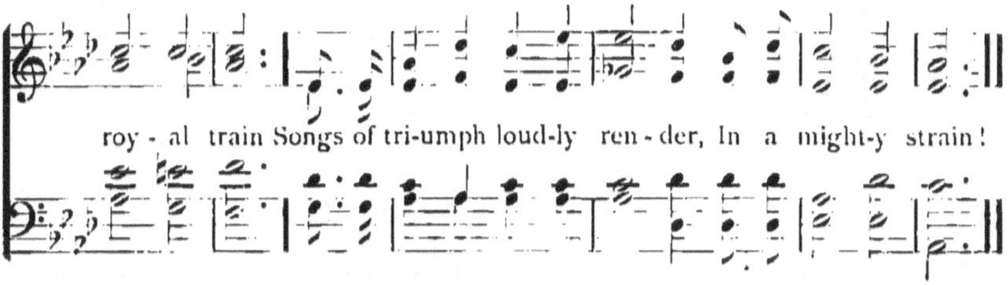

THE LORD'S PRAYER.

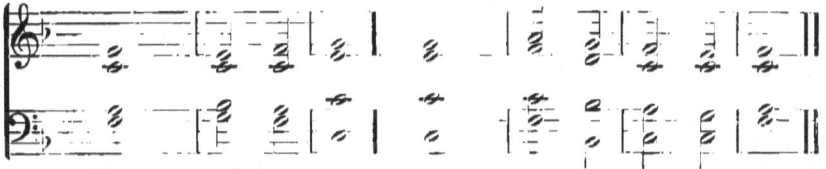

1. Our Father, who art in heaven, hallowed | be Thy | name ;
Thy kingdom come, Thy will be done on | earth, as it | is in | heaven ;
2. Give us this day our | dai-ly | bread ;
And forgive us our trespasses as we forgive those who | tres-pass a-gainst — | us.
3. And lead us not into temptation, but deliver | us from | evil ;
For Thine is the kingdom, and the power, and the glory, for | ever and ever. · A- | men.

3 What sorrows can appall
  When Jesus fills the cup?
  Or should we fear and fall
  While Jesus holds us up?

4 Christ is our life and light,
  Our sunshine never dim,
  Our shelter and our might,
  So we will follow Him.

COPYRIGHT, 1892, BY ASA HULL.

OVER AND OVER AGAIN—Concluded.

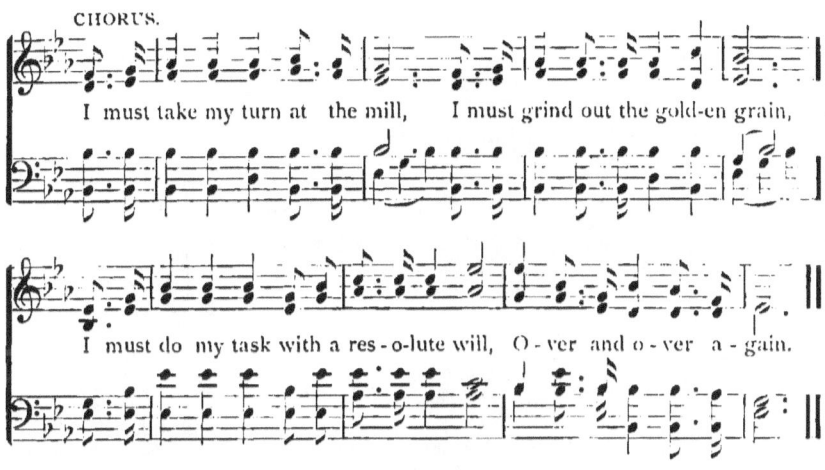

I must take my turn at the mill, I must grind out the gold-en grain,

I must do my task with a res-o-lute will, O-ver and o-ver a-gain.

THE GREAT PHYSICIAN.

Arr. by ASA HULL.   REV. J. H. STOCKTON.

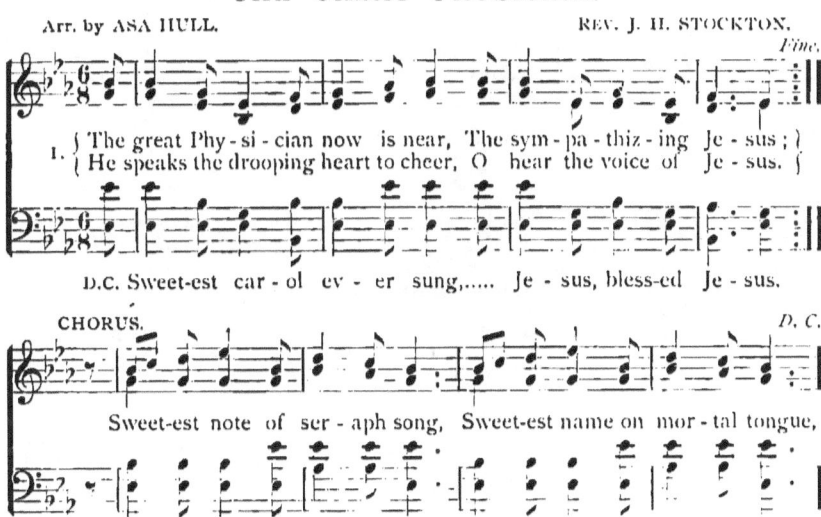

1. { The great Phy-si-cian now is near, The sym-pa-thiz-ing Je-sus;
   { He speaks the drooping heart to cheer, O hear the voice of Je-sus.

D.C. Sweet-est car-ol ev-er sung,...... Je-sus, bless-ed Je-sus.

CHORUS. *D. C.*

Sweet-est note of ser-aph song, Sweet-est name on mor-tal tongue,

2 Your many sins are all forgiven,
   O, hear the voice of Jesus;
   Go on your way in peace to heaven,
   And wear a crown with Jesus.

3 All glory to the dying Lamb!
   I now believe in Jesus;

   I love the blessed Saviour's name,
   I love the name of Jesus.

4 And when to that bright world above,
   We rise to see our Jesus,
   We'll sing around the throne of love
   His name, the name of Jesus.

ALL FOR JESUS.

MARY D. JAMES.   (MIXED VOICES.)   ASA HULL.

1. { All for Je-sus! all for Je-sus! All my being's ransom'd pow'rs; }
   { All my thoughts and words and doings, All my days and all my hours. }
2. { Let my hands perform His bid-ding; Let my feet run in His ways; }
   { Let my eyes see Je-sus on-ly; Let my lips speak forth His praise. }

All for Je-sus! all for Je-sus! All my days and all my hours.
All for Je-sus! all for Je-sus! Let my lips speak forth His praise.

3 Worldlings prize their gems of beauty,
  Cling to gilded toys of dust,
  Boast of wealth, and fame, and pleasure;
    Only Jesus will I trust.
    Only Jesus! only Jesus!
    Only Jesus will I trust.

4 O, what wonder! how amazing!
  Jesus, glorious King of kings,
  Deigns to call me His beloved,
    Lets me rest beneath His wings.
    All for Jesus! all for Jesus!
    Resting now beneath His wings.

COPYRIGHT, 1877, BY ASA HULL.

SON, REMEMBER.

A. W. SPOONER.   REV. A. W. SPOONER.

1. In the land of gath-'ring dark-ness Dives lay in mis-'ry chained;
2. Then he tho't of days long vanished, When he scorned God's warning voice;
3. Loud he called on God for mer-cy, "Fa-ther, pit-y my poor soul!
4. "Son, re-mem-ber," O, re-mem-ber, That to-day is mer-cy's hour;

Round him flashed the fires of tor-ment, Fierce-ly raged, but nev-er waned.
How he turned to paths of pleas-ure, Made the things of earth his choice—
Send me Laz-'rus from Thy bo-som, With one drop of wa-ter cool."
Christ is wait-ing now to par-don, O ac-cept His sav-ing power;

O'er the gulf a-cross which an-gels Nev-er winged their glad-some way,
Of the beg-gar, poor and wretched, Dy-ing at his gate so near,
"Son, re-mem-ber," was the an-swer, "That in life you had your choice,
For, if thou shouldst pass death's por-tals, Unprepared thy doom to meet,

Came these words, in sol-emn ac-cent, From the realms of end-less day.
While the voice, in aw-ful ac-cents, Sound-ed o'er that gulf so clear.
Now in hell art thou for-ev-er, For thou wouldst not hear my voice."
End-less death shall be thy por-tion, Judg-ment mounts the mer-cy-seat.

COPYRIGHT, 1896, BY ASA HULL.

SON, REMEMBER—Concluded. 125

ALL FOR JESUS.

MARY D. JAMES.   (MALE VOICES.)   ASA HULL.

1. All for Jesus! all for Jesus! All my be-ing's ran-som'd pow'rs;
   All my thoughts and words and doings, All my days and all my hours.
2. Let my hands perform His bid-ding; Let my feet run in His ways;
   Let my eyes see Jesus on - ly; Let my lips speak forth His praise.

All for Jesus! all for Jesus! All my days and all my hours.
All for Jesus! all for Jesus! Let my lips speak forth His praise.

3 Worldlings prize their gems of beauty,
   Cling to gilded toys of dust,
Boast of wealth, and fame, and pleasure ;
   Only Jesus will I trust.
      Only Jesus! only Jesus!
      Only Jesus will I trust.

4 O, what wonder! how amazing!
   Jesus, glorious King of kings,
Deigns to call me His beloved,
   Lets me rest beneath His wings.
      All for Jesus! all for Jesus!
      Resting now beneath His wings.

COPYRIGHT, 1873, BY ASA HULL.

I AM THE TRUTH—Concluded.

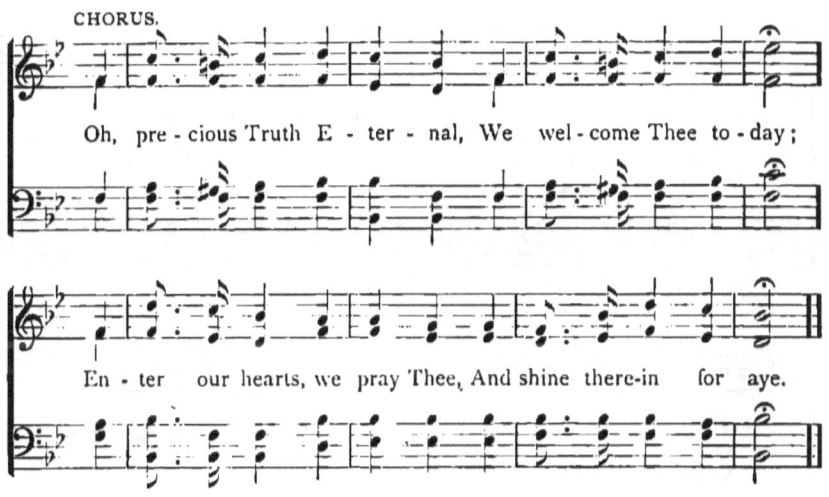

Oh, pre-cious Truth E-ter-nal, We wel-come Thee to-day;
En-ter our hearts, we pray Thee, And shine there-in for aye.

I AM THE LIFE.

WM. EDW. PENNEY. ASA HULL.

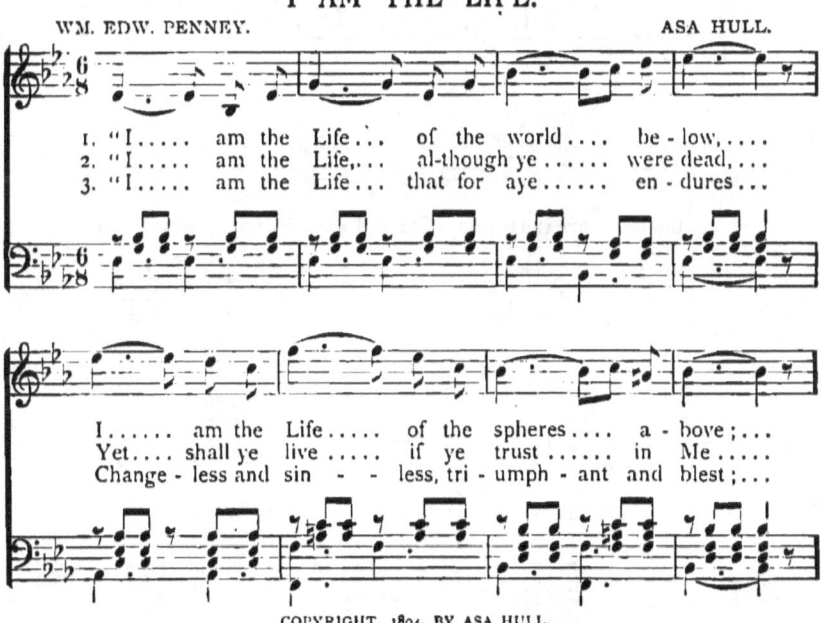

1. "I..... am the Life... of the world.... be-low,....
2. "I..... am the Life,... al-though ye...... were dead,...
3. "I..... am the Life... that for aye...... en-dures...

I...... am the Life..... of the spheres.... a-bove;...
Yet.... shall ye live..... if ye trust...... in Me.....
Change-less and sin- - less, tri-umph-ant and blest;...

COPYRIGHT, 1894, BY ASA HULL.

THANKSGIVING HYMN.   131

E. R. LATTA.　　　　　　　　　　　　　　　　J. E. HALL.

1. For the rich and var-ied blessings, That have throng'd about our way,
2. Gen-tle spring and queenly summer, Each, in turn, their gifts did lay,

In the pass-ing of the sea-sons Let us keep Thanksgiving day.
In the spa-cious lap of au-tumn, To a-dorn this fest-al day.

CHORUS.

To the Au-thor of cre-a-tion Let us now our trib-ute pay;
With the sound of tune-ful voic-es Hail the glad Thanksgiving day.

3 For the sunshine and the showers
　That have wrought this grand display ;
　For the grain, and fruits delicious,
　Let us keep Thanksgiving day.

4 For the friends that still are left us,
　And for hope's inspiring ray,
　With glad hearts, and sunny faces,
　Let us keep this festal day.

COPYRIGHT, 1896, BY ASA HULL.

MY GRACE IS SUFFICIENT—Concluded.

grace .... is suf-fi-cient for thee;... What-ev-er thy
is suf-fi-cient, suf-fi-cient for thee, for thee; What-ev-er thy

bur-den or care, "My grace is suf-fi-cient for thee."

ITALIAN HYMN.

CHARLES WESLEY.   F. GIARDINI.

1. Come, Thou Almighty King, Help us Thy name to sing, Help us to praise; Father all glo-ri-ous, O'er all vic-to-ri-ous, Come and reign o-ver us, An-cient of days.

2 Come Thou Incarnate Word,
Gird on Thy mighty sword,
Our prayer attend;
Come and Thy people bless,
And give Thy word success;
Spirit of holiness,
On us descend.

3 Come, Holy Comforter,
Thy sacred witness bear,
In this glad hour;
Thou who almighty art,
Now rule in every heart,
And ne'er from us depart,
Spirit of power.

ONE DAY NEARER HOME—Concluded.

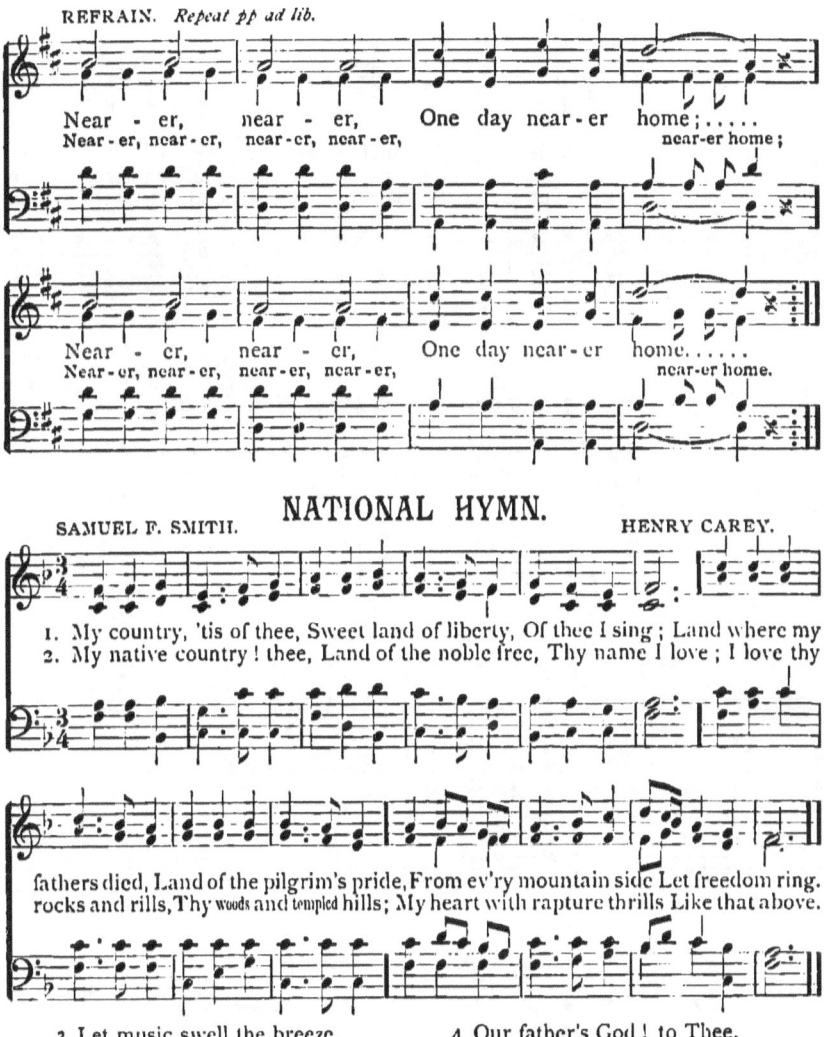

NATIONAL HYMN.

SAMUEL F. SMITH.   HENRY CAREY.

1. My country, 'tis of thee, Sweet land of liberty, Of thee I sing; Land where my fathers died, Land of the pilgrim's pride, From ev'ry mountain side Let freedom ring.
2. My native country! thee, Land of the noble free, Thy name I love; I love thy rocks and rills, Thy woods and templed hills; My heart with rapture thrills Like that above.

3 Let music swell the breeze,
 And ring from all the trees
  Sweet freedom's song !
 Let mortal tongues awake ;
 Let all that breathe partake ;
 Let rocks their silence break ;
  The sound prolong !

4 Our father's God ! to Thee,
 Author of liberty,
  To Thee we sing :
 Long may our land be bright
 With freedom's holy light ;
 Protect us by Thy might,
  Great God, our King !

prais-es to the Lord we sing, Ju-bi-lee, mel-o-dy to our King.

O DAY OF REST.

C. WORDSWORTH.   GERMAN. ARR. BY L. MASON.

1. O day of rest and glad-ness, O day of joy and light!
O balm of care and sad-ness, Most beau-ti-ful, most bright!
On thee, the high and low-ly, Be-fore th' e-ter-nal throne,
Sing Ho-ly! Ho-ly! Ho-ly! To the great Three in One.

2 On thee, at the creation,
   The light first had its birth;
On thee, for our salvation,
   Christ rose from depths of earth,
On thee, our Lord, victorious,
   The Spirit sent from heaven,
And thus on thee most glorious,
   A triple light was given.

3 New graces ever gaining
   From this our day of rest,
We reach the rest remaining
   To spirits of the blest;
To Holy Ghost be praises,
   To Father and to Son;
The Church her voice upraises
   To Thee, blest Three in One.

WHAT DO THE BELLS SAY?

WM. EDW. PENNEY.   ASA HULL.

1. What do the bells in the stee-ple say? Come, O come!...
2. What do the bells to the wea-ry say?
3. What do the bells to the chil-dren say? Come, come, come, O come, O come!

What do the bells to the peo-ple say? Come, O come!...
What do the bells to the sin-ner say?
What do the bells to the teach-er say? Come, come, come, O come, O come!

Come, where dwelleth the Ancient of Days, Just and mer-ci-ful are His ways,
Hearts o'ershadow'd with cankering cares, Sow-ing seed but to gath-er tares,
Here the Lord and His faith-ful ones meet, Here they sit at the Sav-iour's feet,

En-ter in-to His tem-ple with praise, Come, O come!...
Stumbling, fall-ing in pit-falls and snares,
Here is rest and sal-va-tion com-plete, Come, come, come, O come, O come!

COPYRIGHT, 1891, BY ASA HULL.

WHAT DO THE BELLS SAY?—CONCLUDED.

EVEN ME.

1 Lord, I hear of showers of blessing
   Thou art scatt'ring full and free ;
   Showers the thirsty land refreshing ;—
   Let some droppings fall on me,—
     Even me, even me,
   Let some droppings fall on me.

2 Pass me not, O gracious Saviour,
   Let me live and cling to Thee ;
   Fain I'm longing for Thy favor ;
   Whilst Thou'rt calling, call for me ;
     Even me, even me,
   Whilst Thou'rt calling, call for me.

3 Pass me not, O mighty Spirit,
   Thou canst make the blind to see ;
   Witnesses of Jesus' merit,
   Speak some word of power to me ;
     Even me, even me,
   Speak some word of power to me.

4 Pass me not, the lost one bringing,
   Bind my heart, O Lord, to Thee ;
   Whilst the streams of life are springing,
   Blessing others, O bless me ;
     Even me, even me,
   Blessing others, O bless me.

TRYING, EVER TRYING—Concluded.

Try - - ing, Try - ing, ev - er try - ing but the right to do.
Try - ing, ev - er try - ing, Try - - ing but the right to do.

LIFE'S FLOWING RIVER.

J. G. PERCIVAL.   ARR. BY ASA HULL.

1. Faintly flow, thou fall-ing riv - er, Like a dream that dies a - way;
2. Ros-es bloom, and then they wither, Cheeks are bright, then fade and die;

Fine.

Down the o - cean glid-ing ev - er, Keep thy calm, un - ruf - fled way;
D. S. To e - ter - ni - ty's dark o - cean, Bury-ing all its treasures there.
Shapes of light are waft - ed hith - er, Then like vis - ions hur - ry by;
D. S. Time is bear-ing us to heav - en, Home of hap - pi - ness and rest.

D. S.

Time with such a si - lent mo - tion, Floats a - long on wings of air;
Quick as clouds at eve-ning driv - en O'er the man - y col - or'd west,

3 I have read of white robes for the righteous,
    Of bright crowns which the glorified wear,
   When our Father shall bid them "Come, enter,
    And my glory eternally share;"
   How the righteous are evermore blessed
    As they walk through the streets of pure gold;
   But not half of the wonderful story To mortals, etc.

4 I have read of a Christ so forgiving,
    That vile sinners may ask and receive
   Peace and pardon from every transgression,
    If when asking they only believe.
   I have read how He'll guide and protect us,
    If for safety we'll enter His fold;
   But not half of His goodness and mercy To mortals, etc.

144. CHILDREN'S DAY.

G. E. STROBRIDGE, D.D. — ASA HULL.

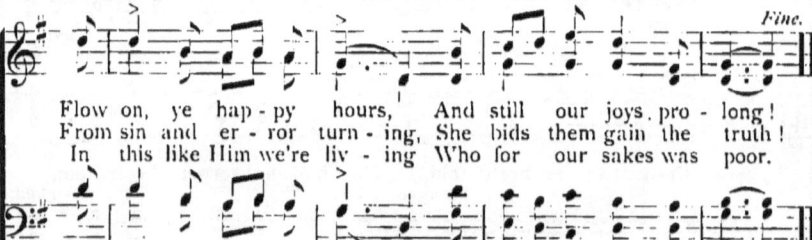

1. All hail! sweet day of flow-ers, Of birds and chil-dren's song!
2. To o-pen founts of learn-ing, Our church in-vites her youth;
3. Nor songs a-lone, but giv-ing, Will Je-sus' smile se-cure:

Cho. All hail! sweet day of flow-ers, Of birds and chil-dren's song!

Flow on, ye hap-py hours, And still our joys pro-long!
From sin and er-ror turn-ing, She bids them gain the truth!
In this like Him we're liv-ing Who for our sakes was poor.

Flow on, ye hap-py hours, And still our joys pro-long!

cres.

As through the heav-ens o'er us, The sun pur-sues his way,
Then crowd the school and col-lege, Heed wis-dom's beck-'ning ray;
We of-fer now our treas-ure, And on His al-tar lay

D. C. for CHORUS.

We'll raise the thrill-ing cho-rus,— Be glad! 'tis Chil-dren's Day!
O may a thirst for knowl-edge Be rous'd this Chil-dren's Day!
Both hearts and gifts with pleas-ure, On this our Chil-dren's Day!

COPYRIGHT, 1884, BY ASA HULL.

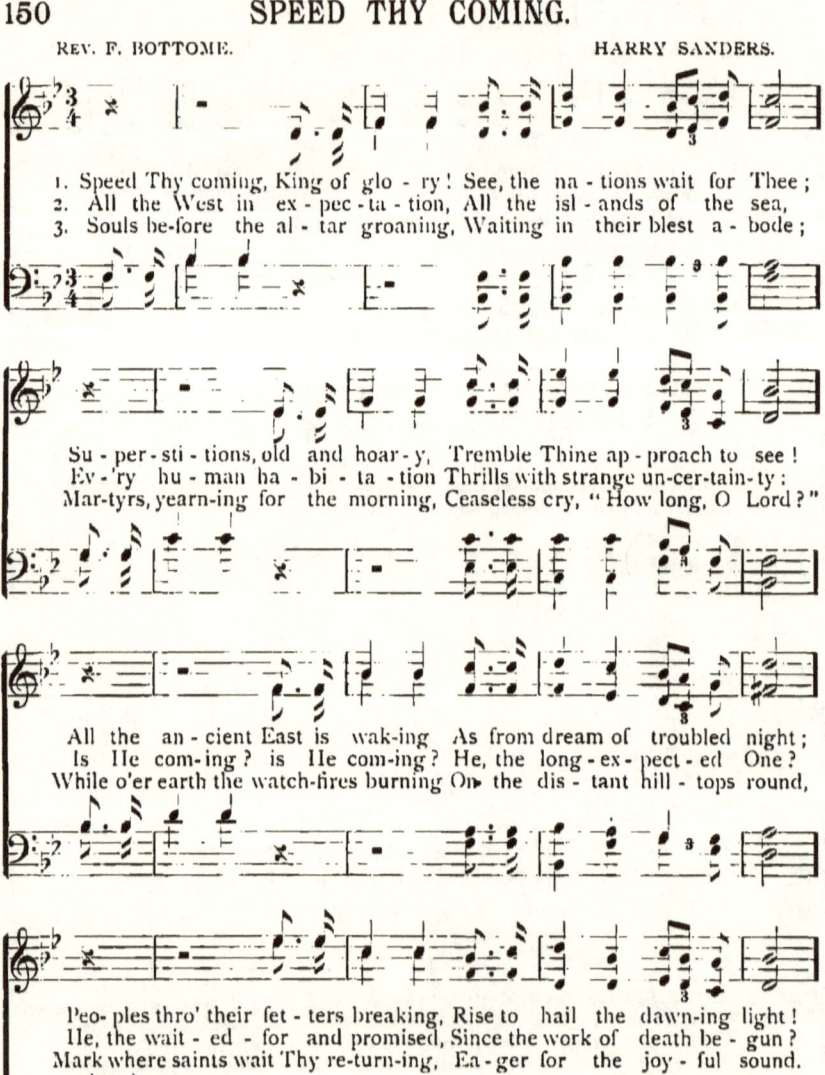

SPEED THY COMING—Concluded.

CHORUS.
He is com-ing in His glo-ry, All the earth shall own His sway;
All the truths of an-cient sto-ry, Cul-mi-nat-ing on that day!

THE SHADES OF EVENING.

C. C. COX. D. E. JONES.

1. Si-lent-ly the shades of ev'-ning Gath-er round my lone-ly door;
   Si-lent-ly they bring be-fore me Fa-ces I shall see no more.
2. Oh, the lost, the un-for-got-ten, Tho' the world be oft for-got;
   Oh, the shroud-ed and the lone-ly, In our hearts they per-ish not.

3 Living in the silent hours,
  Where our spirits only blend;
  They unlinked from earthly trouble,
  We still hoping for its end.

4 How such holy mem'ries cluster,
  Like the stars when storms are past;
  Pointing up to that fair haven,
  We may hope to gain at last.

154. BOYS' BRIGADE HYMN.

WM. EDW. PENNEY.　　　　　　　　　　　　　　　　ASA HULL.
DUET OR UNISON.—*March time.*

1. There's a sound of marching feet, And of bu-gles clear and sweet,
Where for truth and right di-vine Youth is fall-ing in-to line.

2. Mark the camp-fires burning bright, Countless as the stars of night,
Where un-daunt-ed, loy-al youth, Wait-eth to de-fend the truth.

CHORUS.

Forward, march, the Boy's Brigade, May its glo-ry never fade!
the Boy's Brig-ade, the Boy's Brigade, glory nev-er fade, never fade!
May its wav-ing ban-ners be..... Crown'd with joy and vic-to-ry!
be, yes! be

3 Disciplined in heart and hand,
To obey and understand,
Zion's army in reserve
Eager waits her cause to serve.

4 Angel hosts in light arrayed,
Hail with joy the Boy's Brigade ;
Fiends of darkness dread the sight
Of its serried legions bright.

COPYRIGHT, 1896, BY ASA HULL.

ONWARD, CHRISTIAN SOLDIERS. 155

3 Crowns and thrones may perish,
  Kingdoms rise and wane,
But the Church of Jesus
  Constant will remain ;
Gates of hell can never
  'Gainst the Church prevail ;
We have Christ's own promise,
  And that cannot fail.

4 Onward, then, ye people !
  Join our happy throng,
Blend with ours your voices
  In the triumph-song ;
Glory, laud and honor
  Unto Christ, the King ;
This through countless ages
  Men and angels sing.

THE BATTLE MARCH—Concluded.

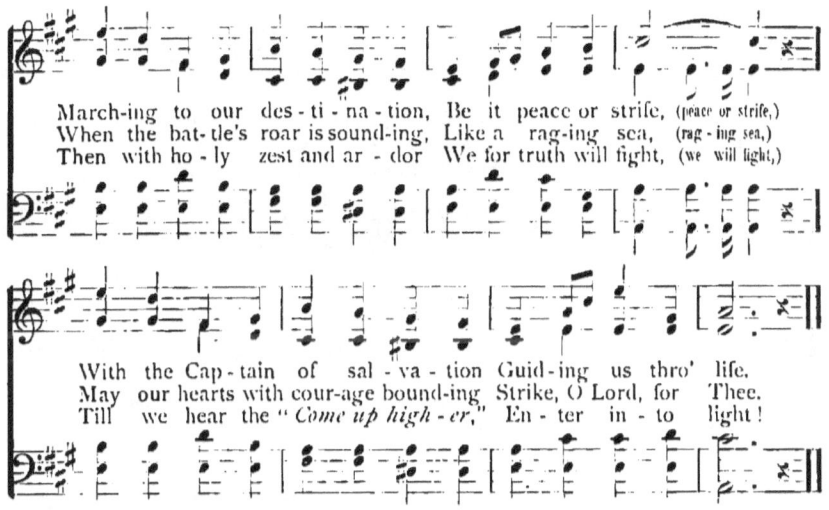

March-ing to our des-ti-na-tion, Be it peace or strife, (peace or strife,)
When the bat-tle's roar is sound-ing, Like a rag-ing sea, (rag-ing sea,)
Then with ho-ly zest and ar-dor We for truth will fight, (we will fight,)

With the Cap-tain of sal-va-tion Guid-ing us thro' life.
May our hearts with cour-age bound-ing Strike, O Lord, for Thee.
Till we hear the "Come up high-er," En-ter in-to light!

THE LOVE OF CHRIST.

A. W. SPOONER. (MALE VOICES.) REV. A. W. SPOONER.

1. The love of Christ to me; How strong that love must be; It brought Him
2. He bore my load of sin, Though spot-less, pure, was He; His pre-cious

down from heav'n To die on Cal-va-ry, To die on Cal-va-ry!
blood was shed That I might ran-somed be, That I might ran-somed be!

3 'Twas I that drove the nails,
And made the thorny crown;
How can He love me so,
||: And claim me for His own?" :||

4 Such love has won my heart,
Blest Saviour, Thou art mine;
O, take me as I am,
||: And keep me ever Thine! :||

COPYRIGHT, 1892, BY ASA HULL.

ON TO VICTORY—Concluded.

Lift ye, then, the glorious banner, Bear it on to victory,
Till the earth has heard the story Of redemption full and free!

ROCK OF AGES.

A. M. TOPLADY. DR. T. HASTINGS.

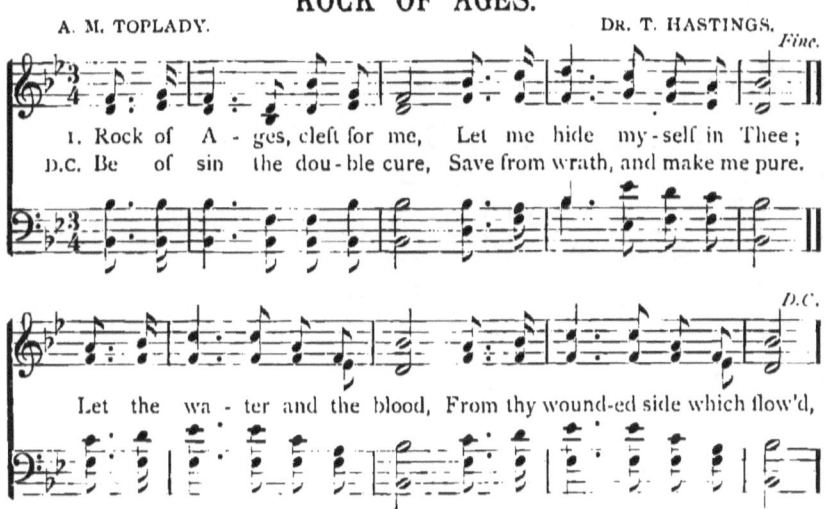

1. Rock of Ages, cleft for me, Let me hide myself in Thee;
D.C. Be of sin the double cure, Save from wrath, and make me pure.
Let the water and the blood, From thy wounded side which flow'd,

2 Could my tears for ever flow,
Could my zeal no languor know,
These for sin could not atone:
Thou must save, and Thou alone:
In my hand no price I bring;
Simply to Thy cross I cling.

3 While I draw this fleeting breath,
When my eyes shall close in death,
When I rise to worlds unknown,
And behold Thee on Thy throne,
Rock of Ages, cleft for me,
Let me hide myself in Thee.

THE BOOK OF THE NEW YEAR. 161

CHAS. EDW. POLLOCK.

1. The book of the New Year is o-pen'd, Its pag-es are spotless and new;
2. And weave for your souls a fair garment Of hon-or and beau-ty and truth,
3. And if on a page you dis-cov-er At ev-'ning a blot or a scrawl,

And so as each leaf-let is turn-ing, Dear scholars, beware what you do!
Which will with a glo-ry en-fold you, When fades the sweet visions of youth;
Kneel quickly and ask the dear Sav-iour In mer-cy to cov-er it all;

Let nev-er a bad thought be cherish'd, Ab-stain from a whisper of guile;
And now, with the new book, endeavor To write its white pages with care;
So, when the strange book shall be finish'd, And closed by the angel of light,

And see that your faces are windows, Thro' which a sweet spirit shall smile.
Each day is a leaf-let, re-mem-ber, To be written with watching and pray'r.
You'll feel, tho' the work is imperfect, You've tried to please God in the right.

COPYRIGHT, 1893, BY ASA HULL.

A HAPPY NEW YEAR—Concluded.

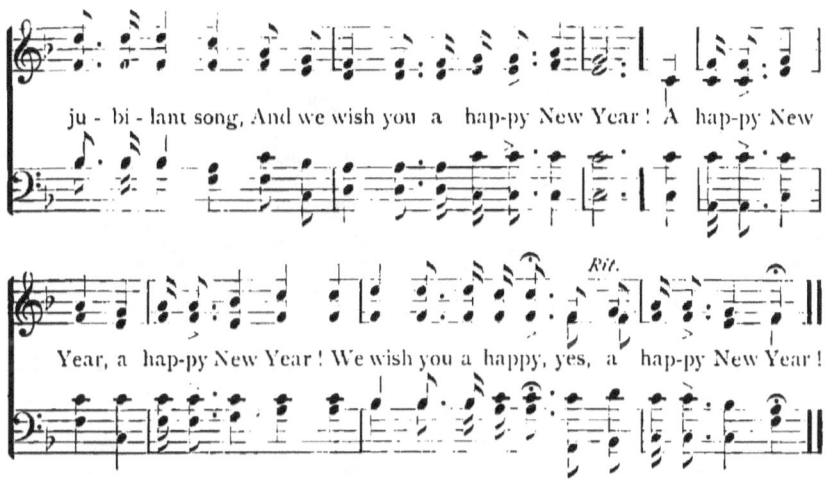

SUN OF MY SOUL.

J. KEBLE.   F. J. HAYDN.

1. Sun of my soul, Thou Saviour dear, It is not night if Thou be near;
O, may no earth-born cloud arise To hide Thee from Thy servant's eyes.

2. When the soft dews of kindly sleep My wearied eye-lids gently steep,
Be my last thought, how sweet to rest For-ev-er on my Saviour's breast.

3 Abide with me from morn till eve,
For without Thee I cannot live;
Abide with me when death is nigh,
For without Thee I dare not die.

4 If some poor wandering child of Thine
Has spurned to-day the voice divine—
Now, Lord, the gracious work begin;
Let him no more lie down in sin.

GOD BE WITH YOU.

165

REV. J. E. RANKIN, D.D.   W. G. TOMER. BY PER.

1. God be with you till we meet again! By His counsels guide, uphold you,
2. God be with you till we meet again! 'Neath His wings securely hide you,
3. God be with you till we meet again! When life's perils thick confound you,
4. God be with you till we meet again! Keep love's banner floating o'er you,

With His sheep securely fold you; God be with you till we meet again!
Dai-ly man-na still provide you; God be with you till we meet again!
Put His loving arms a-round you! God be with you till we meet again!
Smite death's threat'ning wave before you; God be with you till we meet again!

CHORUS.

Till we meet! till we meet! Till we meet at Je-sus' feet!
Till we meet! till we meet again!   till we meet!

Till we meet! till we meet! God be with you till we meet a-gain!
Till we meet! till we meet a-gain!

OUR FESTAL DAY — CONCLUDED.

A - gain.... we sing,... we sing our cheer-ful lay!...
a - gain we sing, we sing, cheer-ful lay!

And praise the Lord who made the flow'rs That glad-den us to - day!

CLINGING TO THE SAVIOUR.

REV. E. H. NEVIN. ASA HULL.

1. O, let me cling to Thee, My Saviour, cling to Thee! When I'm weak and weary,
2. O, let me cling to Thee, My Saviour, cling to Thee! When the winds are blowing,

And my path is drear-y; O, let me cling to Thee, My Saviour, cling to Thee.
And my tears are flowing; O, let me cling to Thee, My Saviour, cling to Thee.

3 O, let me cling to Thee, etc.
   When my friends are leaving,
   And my heart is grieving;
   O, let me cling to Thee, etc.

4 O, let me cling to Thee, etc.
   When I cross the river,
   Which from earth doth sever,
   O, let me cling to Thee, etc.

168. HOSANNA IN THE HIGHEST.

W. J. KIRKPATRICK.

1. What are those soul-reviving strains Which echo thus from Salem's plains?
2. Lo! 'tis a youth-ful chorus sings, Ho-san-na to the King of kings;
3. Mes - si - ah's name shall joy im-part A - like to Jew and Gen-tile heart:
4. Pro-claim ho-san-nas loud and clear; See Da-vid's Son and Lord ap-pear!

What anthems loud, and louder still, So sweet-ly sound from Zi - on's hill?
Nor these alone their voice shall raise, For we will join this song of praise.
He bled for us, He bled for you, And we will sing ho - san - na too.
All praise on earth to Him be giv'n, And glory shout through highest heav'n.

CHORUS.

Ho - san - na in the high - est, Ho - san - na in the high - est,

Bless-ed is He that cometh in the name of the Lord, Blessed is He that

COPYRIGHT, 1876, BY ASA HULL.

HARK! FROM THE MIDNIGHT HILLS.
(For the foregoing Music.)

1 Hark! from the midnight hills around,
A voice of more than mortal sound,
In distant hallelujahs stole,
Wild murm'ring o'er the raptured soul.

2 On wings of light, on wings of flame,
The glorious hosts of Zion came;
High heaven with songs of triumph rung
While thus they struck their harps and sung:

3 "O Zion, lift thy raptured eye;
The long-expected hour is nigh;
The joys of nature rise again;
The Prince of Salem comes to reign.

4 He comes to cheer the trembling heart;
Bids Satan and his host depart;
Again the day-star gilds the gloom;
Again the bowers of Eden bloom."

EASTER OFFERINGS—Concluded.

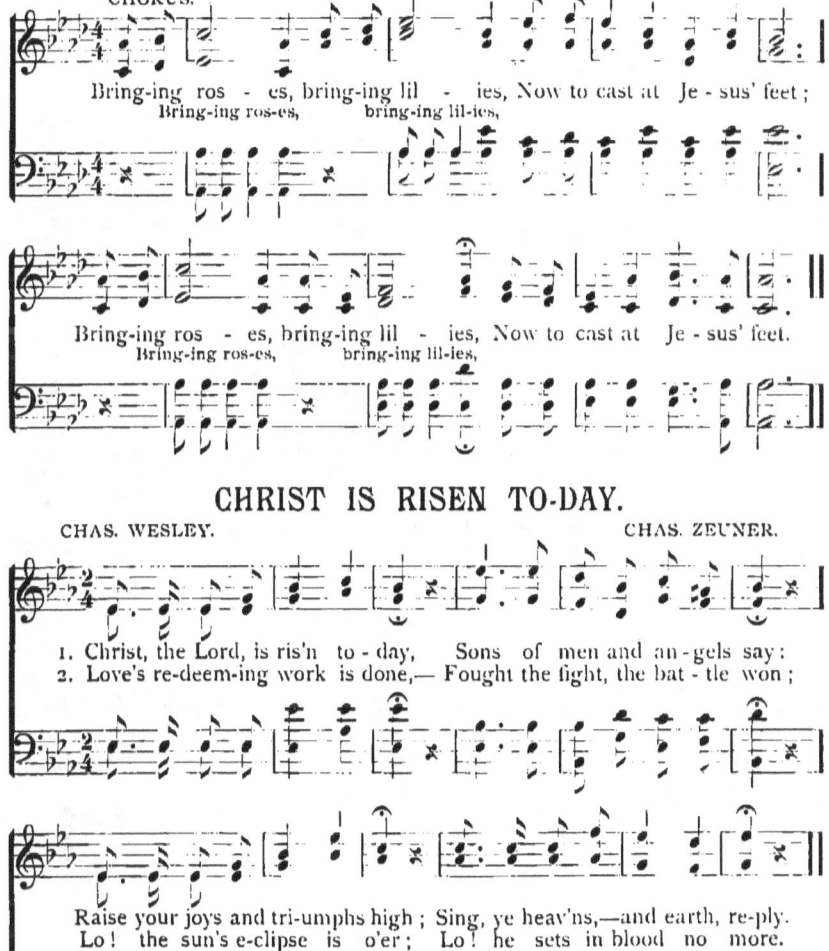

CHRIST IS RISEN TO-DAY.

CHAS. WESLEY.   CHAS. ZEUNER.

1. Christ, the Lord, is ris'n to-day, Sons of men and an-gels say;
2. Love's re-deem-ing work is done,— Fought the fight, the bat-tle won;

Raise your joys and tri-umphs high; Sing, ye heav'ns,—and earth, re-ply.
Lo! the sun's e-clipse is o'er; Lo! he sets in blood no more.

3 Vain the stone, the watch, the seal;
  Christ has burst the gates of hell;
  Death in vain forbids His rise;
  Christ hath opened Paradise.

4 Lives again our glorious King;
  Where, O death, is now thy sting?
  Once He died our souls to save;
  Where's thy vict'ry, boasting grave?

174. GLORY IN THE HIGHEST.

LANTA WILSON SMITH.　　　　　　　　　　　HARRY SANDERS.

1. While the shep-herds in the mid-night Watched their flocks on Judah's plains,
2. Un-to you a child is giv-en— Bless-ed Sav-iour, Prince of Peace—
3. Not a-lone to watch-ing shepherds Came the glo-ry in the night,
4. And like those who bro't their treasure To the man-ger-cra-dled King,

Lo! a glo-ry shone from heav-en, Min-gled with a glad re-frain.
Bring-ing joy to ev-'ry na-tion, And to cap-tive souls re-lease.
It has float-ed down the a-ges, Fill-ing all the world with light.
We to-night our love may of-fer, We our hearts best treas-ures bring.

REFRAIN.

Glo - ry in the high - est, Glo - - - - - ry!
　　　　　　　　　　　　　　Glo - ry in the high - est,
Glo - ry in the high - est, Glo - - - - - ry!
　　　　　　　　　　　　　　Glo - ry in the high - est!

COPYRIGHT, 1896, BY ASA HULL.

RING OUT THE BELLS—CONCLUDED. 179

CHORUS.

Ring out the bells for Christmas, Ring out the bells for Christmas,
Ring out the bells Ring out the bells
Ring out the bells, Ring out the bells, The hap-py, hap-py day!
Ring out the bells, Ring out the bells,

MARTYN.

C. WESLEY.   S. B. MARSH. ARR.

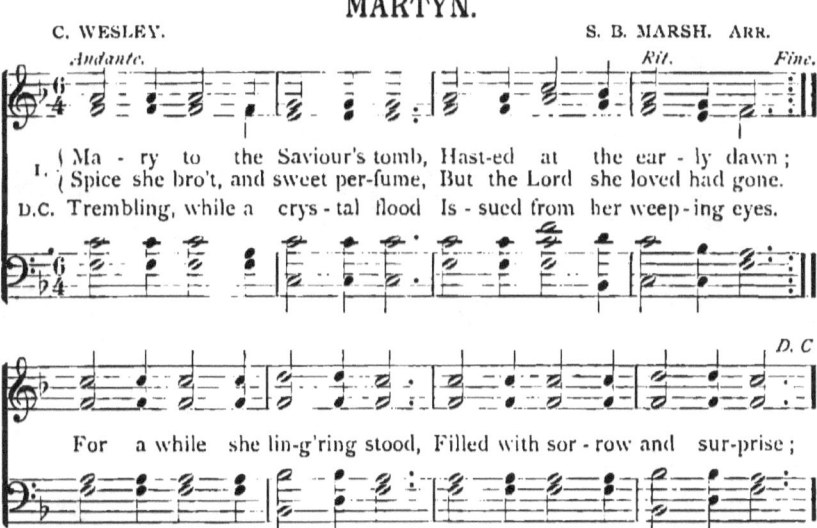

1. { Ma - ry to the Saviour's tomb, Hast-ed at the ear - ly dawn;
  { Spice she bro't, and sweet per-fume, But the Lord she loved had gone.
D.C. Trembling, while a crys - tal flood Is - sued from her weep-ing eyes.

For a while she lin-g'ring stood, Filled with sor - row and sur-prise;

2 But her sorrow quickly fled,   What a change His word can make,
  When she heard His welcome voice;   Turning darkness into day!
  Christ had risen from the dead;   Ye who weep for Jesus' sake,
  Now He bids her heart rejoice.   He will wipe your tears away.

4 And so to-night I almost know
   The very things he's brought below,
   And hung upon that Christmas tree
   Because he is so good to me.

5 But now, no more my song I'll sing,
   For I can hear his sleigh-bells ring,
   And Santa soon will give to me
   My things from off this Christmas tree.

[Santa makes his appearance while last chorus is being sung.]

CHRISTMAS MUSIC.

181

MARIAN FROELICH. G. FROELICH.

1. Christmas mu-sic mer-ri-ly wakes the ech-oes; Hark! hark! how it freights the air;
2. Christmas mu-sic mer-ri-ly wakes the ech-oes; Hark! hark! o'er the cit-y's streets;
3. Christmas mu-sic mer-ri-ly wakes the ech-oes; Hark! hark! sounding far and near;

While the storm-king holds its wild-est rev-els, Flings, flings snow-drifts ev-ery-where;
Peal-ing clear-ly while the snow is fall-ing, Pure, pure, cov-'ring all it meets;
Hap-py chil-dren lend their flute-like voices, Praise, praise Christmas joy and cheer;

From the bel-fry in the tow-er, In the chap-el on the hill,
The ca-the-dral's deep-toned thun-der Joins a sweet-ly chim-ing bell,
Sweet-est mu-sic of the heart-strings, Swept by fin-gers skilled by love,

Har-mo-ny de-scends like sil-ver show-er, Or like sweet-ly flow-ing rill.
And the pass-er, lost in joy and won-der, Lists what met-al tongues can tell.
Gives to life a charm so true, en-dear-ing, Earth be-comes like heav'n a-bove.

COPYRIGHT, 1883, BY ASA HULL.

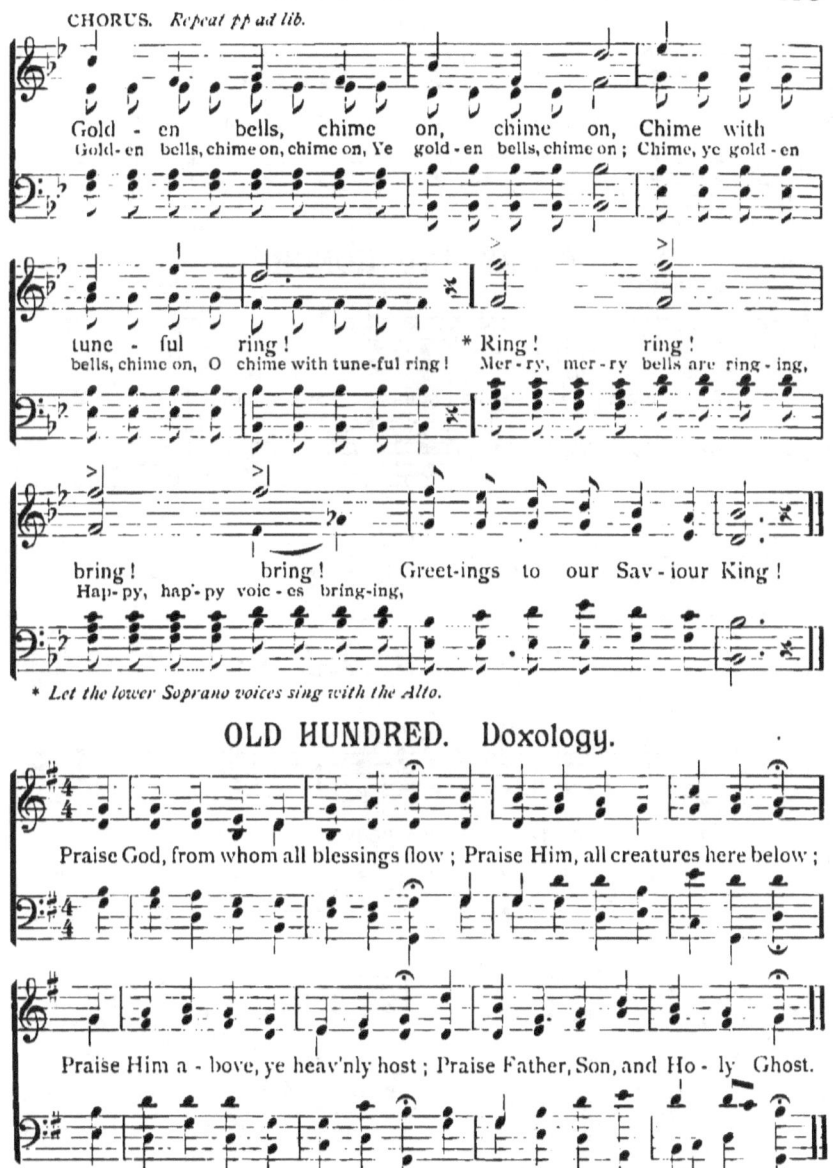

ORDERS OF EXERCISES FOR SESSION.

Order, No. 1.
Opening.

1. SALUTATION.—*Matt.* xi. 28.
Supt. Come unto me all ye that labor and are heavy laden and I will give you rest. Take my yoke upon you, and learn of me; for I am meek and lowly in heart and ye shall find find rest unto your souls.
2. SINGING. (*To be selected.*)
3. SCRIPTURE SELECTIONS.

Supt. Ho, every one that thirsteth, come ye to the waters, and he that hath no money, come ye, buy and eat, yea, come, buy wine and milk without money and without price.

Teachers. Wherefore do ye spend money for that which is not bread, and your labor for that which satisfyeth not?

Scholars. Hearken diligently unto me, and eat ye that which is good, and let your soul delight itself in fatness.

Supt. Seek ye the Lord while he may be found; call ye upon him while he is near.

Teachers. Let the wicked forsake his way and the unrighteous man his thoughts.

Scholars. And let him return unto the Lord, and he will have mercy upon him; and to our God for he will abundantly pardon.—*Isaiah* lv. 1, 2, 6, 7.

4. PRAYER. (*Closing with Lord's Prayer.**)
5. SINGING. (*To be selected.*)

Lesson.

6. READING THE LESSON RESPONSIVELY.
7. STUDYING THE LESSON IN CLASSES.
8. LESSON REVIEW BY SUPT.

Closing.

9. REPORT OF ATTENDANCE.
10. ANNOUNCEMENTS.
11. SINGING. (*To be selected.*)
12. SCRIPTURE SELECTIONS.

Supt. The Lord bless thee and keep thee.

Teachers. The Lord make his face shine upon thee, and be gracious to thee.

Scholars. The Lord lift up his countenance upon thee and give the peace.
—*Numbers* vi. 24—26.

13. DISMISSION.

Order, No. 2.
Opening.

1. SALUTATION.—*Psalm* cxix. 105.
Supt. Thy word is a lamp unto my feet and a light unto my path.
2. SINGING. (*To be selected.*)
3. SCRIPTURE SELECTIONS.

Supt. Search the Scriptures: for in them ye think ye have eternal life. And they are they which testify of me.—*John* v. 39.

Teachers. All Scripture is given by inspiration of God, and is profitable for doctrine, for reproof, for correction, for instruction in righteousness.

Scholars. That the man of God may be perfect, thoroughly furnished unto all good works.—2 *Tim.* iii. 16, 17.

Supt. Open thou mine eyes, that I may behold wondrous things out of thy law.

Teachers. The entrance of thy words giveth light; it giveth understanding unto the simple.—*Psalm* cxix. 18, 130.

Scholars. Teach me thy way, O Lord; I will walk in thy truth; unite my heart to fear thy name.—*Psalm* lxxxvi. 11.

4. PRAYER. (*Closing with Lord's Prayer.**)
5. SINGING. (*To be selected.*)

Lesson.

6. READING THE LESSON RESPONSIVELY.
7. STUDYING THE LESSON IN CLASSES.
8. LESSON REVIEW BY SUPT.

Closing.

9. REPORT OF ATTENDANCE.
10. ANNOUNCEMENTS.
11. SINGING. (*To be selected.*)
12. SCRIPTURE SELECTIONS.

Supt. The law of the Lord is perfect, converting the soul; the testimony of the Lord is sure, making wise the simple.

Teachers. The statutes of the Lord are right, rejoicing the heart; the commandment of the Lord is pure, enlightening the eyes.

Scholars. More to be desired are they than gold, yea, than much fine gold; sweeter also than honey and the honeycomb.
—*Psalm* xix. 7, 8, 10.

13. DISMISSION.

ORDERS OF EXERCISES—CONTINUED.

Order, No. 3.
Opening.
1. SALUTATION.—*Psalm* xix. 14.
Supt. Let the words of my mouth and the meditation of my heart be acceptable in thy sight, O Lord, my strength and my redeemer.
2. SINGING. (*To be selected.*)
3. SCRIPTURE SELECTIONS.
Supt. Blessed is the man that walketh not in the counsel of the ungodly, nor standeth in the way of sinners, nor sitteth in the seat of the scornful.
Teachers. But his delight is in the law of the Lord, and in his law doth he meditate day and night.
Scholars. And he shall be like a tree planted by the rivers of water, that bringeth forth his fruit in his season; his leaf also shall not wither; and whatsoever he doeth shall prosper.
Supt. The ungodly are not so; but are like the chaff which the wind driveth away.
Teachers. Therefore the ungodly shall not stand in the judgment, nor sinners in the congregation of the righteous.
Scholars. For the Lord knoweth the way of the righteous, but the way of the ungodly shall perish.—*Psalm* i.
4. PRAYER. (*Closing with Lord's Prayer.*)
5. SINGING. (*To be selected.*)

Lesson.
6. READING THE LESSON RESPONSIVELY.
7. STUDYING THE LESSON IN CLASSES.
8. LESSON REVIEW BY SUPT.

Closing.
9. REPORT OF ATTENDANCE.
10. ANNOUNCEMENTS.
11. SINGING. (*To be selected.*)
12. SCRIPTURE SELECTIONS.
Supt. Blessed are they that do his commandments, that they may have right to the tree of life, and may enter in through the gates into the city.
Teachers. And the Spirit and the bride say, Come. And let him that heareth say, Come.
Scholars. And let him that is athirst come, and whosoever will let him take the water of life freely.—*Rev.* xxii. 14, 17.
13. DISMISSION.

Order, No. 4.
Opening.
1. SALUTATION.—*Psalm* cxlv. 15, 16.
Supt. The eyes of all wait upon thee and thou givest them their meat in due season. Thou openest thy hand and satisfiest the desire of every living thing.
2. SINGING. (*To be selected.*)
3. SCRIPTURE SELECTIONS.
Supt. Make a joyful noise unto the Lord, all ye lands.
Teachers. Serve the Lord with gladness; come before his presence with singing.
Scholars. Know ye that the Lord he is God; it is he that hath made us, and not we ourselves; we are his people and the sheep of his pasture.
Supt. Enter into his gates with thanksgiving, and into his courts with praise.
Teachers. Be thankful unto him, and bless his name.
Scholars. For the Lord is good; his mercy is everlasting; and his truth endureth to all generations.—*Psalm* c.
4. PRAYER. (*Closing with Lord's Prayer.*)
5. SINGING. (*To be selected.*)

Lesson.
6. READING THE LESSON RESPONSIVELY.
7. STUDYING THE LESSON IN CLASSES.
8. LESSON REVIEW BY SUPT.

Closing.
9. REPORT OF ATTENDANCE.
10. ANNOUNCEMENTS.
11. SINGING. (*To be selected.*)
12. SCRIPTURE SELECTIONS.
Supt. God be merciful unto us and bless us, and cause his face to shine upon us.
Teachers. That thy way may be known upon earth, thy saving health among all nations.
Scholars. Then shall the earth yield her increase, and God, even our own God, shall bless us.—*Psalm* lxvii. 1, 2, 6.
13. DISMISSION.

ORDERS OF EXERCISES--CONTINUED.

No. 5. Missionary.
Opening.
1. SALUTATION.—*Isaiah* lii. 7.

Supt. How beautiful upon the mountains are the feet of him that bringeth good tidings, that publisheth peace; that bringeth good tidings of good, that publisheth salvation; that saith unto Zion, Thy God reigneth.

2. SINGING. (*To be selected.*)
3. SCRIPTURE SELECTIONS.

Supt. Go ye therefore and teach all nations, baptizing them in the name of the Father and of the Son and of the Holy Ghost.

Teachers. Teaching them to observe all things whatsoever I have commanded you;

Scholars. And lo! I am with you always, even unto the end of the world.
Matt. xxviii. 19, 20.

Supt. And the Gentiles shall come to thy light and kings to the brightness of thy rising.—*Isaiah* lx. 3.

Teachers. I will declare the decree; the Lord hath said unto me, Thou art my Son; this day have I begotten thee.

Scholars. Ask of me and I shall give thee the heathen for thine inheritance, and the uttermost parts of the earth for thy possession.—*Psalm* ii. 7, 8.

4. PRAYER. (*Closing with Gloria Patri.**)
5. SINGING. (*To be selected.*)

Lesson.
6. READING THE LESSON RESPONSIVELY.
7. STUDYING THE LESSON IN CLASSES.
8. LESSON REVIEW BY SUPT.

Closing.
9. REPORT OF ATTENDANCE.
10. ANNOUNCEMENTS.
11. SINGING. (*To be selected.*)
12. SCRIPTURE SELECTIONS.

Supt. Say not ye there are four months, and then cometh harvest; behold, I say unto you, Lift up your eyes and look on the fields, for they are white already to harvest.

Teachers. And he that reapeth receiveth wages, and gathereth fruit unto life eternal.

Scholars. That both he that soweth and he that reapeth may rejoice together.
John iv. 35, 36.

13. DISMISSION.

No. 6. Benevolence.
Opening.
1. SALUTATION.—*Exodus* xxxv. 5.

Supt. Take ye from among you an offering unto the Lord, whosoever is of a willing heart, let him bring it, an offering of the Lord.

2. SINGING. (*To be selected.*)
3. SCRIPTURE SELECTIONS.

Supt. Every man according as he purposeth in his heart, so let him give; not grudgingly or of necessity, for God loveth a cheerful giver.—2 *Cor.* ix. 7.

Teachers. And let us not be weary in well-doing for in due season we shall reap if we faint not.

Scholars. As we have therefore opportunity let us do good unto all men,

Supt. Especially unto them who are of the household of faith.—*Gal.* vi. 9, 10.

Teachers. I have showed you all things, how that so laboring ye ought to support the weak,

Scholars. And to remember the words of the Lord Jesus, how he said, It is more blessed to give than to receive.—*Acts* xx. 35.

4. PRAYER. (*Closing with Gloria Patri.**)
5. SINGING. (*To be selected.*)

Lesson.
6. READING THE LESSON RESPONSIVELY.
7. STUDYING THE LESSON IN CLASSES.
8. LESSON REVIEW BY SUPT.

Closing.
9. REPORT OF ATTENDANCE.
10. ANNOUNCEMENTS.
11. SINGING. (*To be selected.*)
12. SCRIPTURE SELECTIONS.

Supt. Take heed that ye do not your alms before men to be seen of them; otherwise ye have no reward of your Father which is in heaven.

Teachers. But when thou doest alms, let not thy left hand know what thy right hand doeth.

Scholars. That thine alms may be in secret; and thy Father which seeth in secret, himself shall reward thee openly.
Matt. vi. 1, 3, 4.

13. DISMISSION.

ORDERS OF EXERCISES—Concluded.

No. 7. Greeting.
Opening.
1. SALUTATION.—*Psalm* xxvii. 4.
   Supt. One thing have I desired of the Lord, that will I seek after; that I may dwell in the house of the Lord all the days of my life, to behold the beauty of the Lord, and to inquire in his temple.
2. SINGING. (*To be selected.*)
3. SCRIPTURE SELECTIONS.
   Supt. How amiable are thy tabernacles, O Lord of Hosts!
   Teachers. My soul longeth, yea, even fainteth for the courts of the Lord; my heart and my flesh crieth out for the living God.
   Scholars. Yea, the sparrow hath found a house, and the swallow a nest for herself where she may lay her young, even thine altars, O Lord of hosts, my King and my God.
   Supt. Blessed are they that dwell in thy house; they will be still praising thee.
   Teachers. For a day in thy courts is better than a thousand.
   Scholars. I had rather be a doorkeeper in the house of my God than to dwell in the tents of wickedness.—*Psalm* lxxxiv. 1-4, 10.
4. PRAYER. (*Closing with Gloria Patri.**)
5. SINGING. (*To be selected.*)

Lesson.
6. READING THE LESSON RESPONSIVELY.
7. STUDYING THE LESSON IN CLASSES.
8. LESSON REVIEW BY SUPT.

Closing.
9. REPORT OF ATTENDANCE.
10. ANNOUNCEMENTS.
11. SINGING. (*To be selected.*)
12. SCRIPTURE SELECTIONS.
    Supt. I was glad when they said unto me, Let us go into the house of the Lord.
    Teachers. Our feet shall stand within thy gates, O Jerusalem.
    Scholars. Peace be within thy walls and prosperity within thy palaces.
    Psalm cxxii. 1, 2, 7.
13. DISMISSION.

No. 8. Temperance.
Opening.
1. SALUTATION.—*Prov.* xx. 1.
   Supt. Wine is a mocker, strong drink is raging; and whosoever is deceived thereby is not wise.
2. SINGING. (*To be selected.*)
3. SCRIPTURE SELECTIONS.
   Supt. Be not among wine-bibbers; among riotous eaters of flesh.
   Teachers. For the drunkard and the glutton shall come to poverty, and drowsiness shall clothe a man with rags.
   Scholars. Who hath woe? who hath sorrow? who hath contentions? who hath babbling? who hath wounds without cause? who hath redness of eyes?
   Supt. They that tarry long at the wine; they that go to seek mixed wine.
   Teachers. Look not thou upon the wine when it is red, when it giveth its colour in the cup, when it moveth itself aright;
   Scholars. At the last it biteth like a serpent and stingeth like an adder.
   Prov. xxiii. 19, 20, 29-31.
4. PRAYER. (*Closing with Gloria Patri.**)
5. SINGING. (*To be selected.*)

Lesson.
6. READING THE LESSON RESPONSIVELY.
7. STUDYING THE LESSON IN CLASSES.
8. LESSON REVIEW BY SUPT.

Closing.
9. REPORT OF ATTENDANCE.
10. ANNOUNCEMENTS.
11. SINGING. (*To be selected.*)
12. SCRIPTURE SELECTIONS.
    Supt. And be not drunk with wine wherein is excess, but be filled with the Spirit.
    Eph. v. 18.
    Teachers. Woe unto them that rise up early in the morning that they may follow strong drink.
    Scholars. That continue until night till wine inflame them.—*Isaiah* v. 11.
13. DISMISSION.

* Note.—The *Lord's Prayer* can be chanted, see page 117, or repeated in concert. Two selections for *Gloria Patri*, pages 77 and 89, are given. "Glory and Honor," page 184, is appropriate in "Order No. 4," when used for a Thanksgiving or Praise Service. "Bow down Thine ear," same page, can be substituted for the *Lord's Prayer* or *Gloria Patri*, when desired.

INDEX OF TUNES.

A
	PAGE
A happy New Year	162
All for Jesus (mixed voices)	123
All for Jesus (male voices)	125
All Glory to the Lamb	28
A Song of Joy	82
At the Setting of the Sun	54

B
Beacon Lights are shining	31
Beyond the Shadows	50
Blessed Assurance	59
Blessed Master, send me	39
Blest be the Tie	37
Bought with a Price	84
Bow down Thine Ear	184
Boys' Brigade Hymn	154
By cool Siloam's shady Rill	17

C
Call to Prayer	44
Can the Lord depend on you?	76
Children's Day	144
Christ is risen to-day	171
Christmas Music	181
Christ our Friend	57
Chose ye, one and all	64
Clinging to the Saviour	167
Closer to Thee	98
Come unto Me	24
Coming to the Cross	79
Coronation	97
Crown, Harp and Song	80

D
Dear Lord, remember me	85

E
Easter Offerings	170
Earnest Toilers	6
Echoes from Bethlehem	176
Even me	139
Eventide	81
Ever Press onward	75

F
Fair Galilee	112
Far out on the lonely Billow	23
Follow the Flag of Jesus	67
Forget me not	43
From o'er the Sea	60

G
Give me the World for Jesus	96
Gloria Patri, No. 1	77

	PAGE
Gloria Patri, No. 2	89
Glory and Honor	184
Glory in the Highest	174
God be with you	165
God's wondrous Love	21
Golden Bells	182
Golden Doors	177
Good-bye, good-bye	25
Good-night, but not Farewell	164

H
Hark! from the Midnight Hills	169
He calleth for thee	22
Higher, ever higher	13
His folded Wing	19
Holy, Lord God Almighty	9
Hosanna in the Highest	168

I
I am the Door	126
I am the Life	129
I am the Truth	128
I am the Way	127
I cannot keep from Singing	66
I heard His call	100
Inside the Gate	48
In the glad some Day	102
In the King's Highway	34
It all will be bright	12
Italian Hymn	133
I will praise my dear Redeemer	11

J
Jerusalem the Golden	111
Jesus calls for Workers	46
Jesus died for you	101
Jesus is calling	65
Jesus is mine	105
Jesus knows all about it	26
Jesus loves little Children	61
Jesus, our Guide	119
Jesus, Refuge of my soul	51
Jesus, Saviour, pilot me	33
Joy to the World	175
Just as I am	113

K
Keep straight ahead	58

L
Lead, kindly Light	149
Lessons of Nature	7
Life's flowing River	141
Like a sparkling River	3

INDEX OF TUNES.

M
	PAGE
Marching to the Land above	146
Martyn	179
My blessed Redeemer	27
My Grace is sufficient	132

N
National Hymn	135
No Book is like the Bible	103
Not half has ever been told	142

O
O Day of Rest	137
Oh, to be Something	32
Old Hundred (Doxology)	183
Olivet	93
On an Easter Morning	172
One Day nearer Home	134
On to Victory	158
Onward, Christian Soldiers	155
Onward, right onward	49
O, think of a Home over there	63
Our festal Day	166
Our Offering bring	53
Over and over again	120

P
Practice what you preach	18

R
Rejoice and be glad	99
Rest and talk with Jesus	30
Resting in the Sunlight	86
Resting, sweetly resting	122
Ring out the Bells	178
Rock of Ages	159
Roll away the Stone	87

S
Sail not without the Master	94
Save and comfort me	35
Saviour, Refuge	91
Scatter Sunshine and Gladness	42
Seasons	69
Seek Him to-day	72
Singing for Jesus	15
Sitting at His Feet	10
Some Day, yes, some Day	71
Something every Day	104
Sometime	153
Songs of Jubilee	136
Son, remember	124
Sound the Battle-Cry	107
Sowing Seeds of Good or Ill	56

	PAGE
Speed Thy coming	150
Stand up for Jesus	148
Stop a Moment and think	14
Sun of my Soul	163
Sweet Zion Bells	45

T
Tell that I'm coming to Jesus	83
Tenderly calling	74
Thanksgiving Hymn	131
Thanks to Thee, our Father	160
The Anchor of Hope	118
The Ark of Salvation	110
The Armor of God	62
The Battle March	156
The Book of the New Year	161
The Border Line	109
The Christian Soldier	20
The Christmas Tree	180
The City of God	90
The Golden Shore	5
The Gospel's Triumph	4
The Great Physician	121
The Handwriting on the Wall	114
The Harbor Light	106
The Hills of Amethyst	47
The Home beyond	68
The King's Advance	116
The Light of Love	40
The Lord's Prayer (Chant)	117
The Love of Christ	157
The Middle of the King's Highway	38
The Sabbath School	108
The Shades of Evening	151
The Temperance Banner	95
The Toilers' Song	36
There is Room for all	73
There's Room at the Feast	92
Trust and try	8
Trusting in the Ark	29
Trying, ever trying	140

W
Walk in the Light	70
Watch and pray	88
Welcome Greeting	145
We'll take the World for Jesus	152
What a Friend we have in Jesus	55
What do the Bells say?	138
When we reach the Gates of Gold	16
Where the Gates are open	78
Whiter than Snow	52
Who is He in Light arrayed?	173
Wonderful Riches	40

INDEX OF SUBJECTS.

Anniversary.

	PAGE
Boys' Brigade Hymn	154
Marching to the Land above	146
Onward, Christian Soldiers	155
The King's Advance	116
Welcome Greeting	145
We'll take the World for Jesus	152

Children's Day.
(See also Anniversary.)

Children's Day	144
Hosanna in the Highest	168
Jesus loves little Children	61
Our Festal Day	166
Songs of Jubilee	136
The Battle March	156

Christmas.

Christmas Music	181
Echoes from Bethlehem	176
Glory in the Highest	174
Golden Bells	182
Golden Doors	177
Joy to the World	175
Ring out the Bells	178
The Christmas Tree	180

Devotional.
(See also Familiar Hymns.)

All for Jesus	123
Blessed Assurance	59
Clinging to the Saviour	167
Closer to Thee	98
Far out on the lonely Billow	23
His folded Wing	19
Jesus knows all about it	26
My blessed Redeemer	27
Resting, sweetly resting	122
Save and comfort me	35
Saviour, Refuge	91
Singing for Jesus	15
Sitting at His Feet	10
Whiter than Snow	52

Easter.

Christ is risen to-day	171
Easter Offerings	170
Martyn	179
On an Easter Morning	172
Who is He in Light arrayed?	173

Encouragement and Cheer.

A Song of Joy	82
Crown, Harp and Song	80
Higher, ever higher	13
I cannot keep from singing	66
It all will be bright	12
Keep straight ahead	58
Rejoice and be glad	99
Stop a moment and think	14
The Armor of God	62
Trust and try	8

Heaven.

Inside the Gate	48
In the glad some Day	102
Jerusalem the Golden	111
The Border Line	109
The Golden Shore	5
The Home beyond	68
When we reach the Gates of Gold	16
Where the Gates are open	78

Invitation.

Bought with a Price	84
Come unto Me	24
Seek Him to-day	72
Son, remember	124
Tenderly calling	74
There is Room for all	73
There's Room at the Feast	92

Missionary.

Blessed Master, send me	39
Give me the World for Jesus	96
Jesus calls for Workers	46
Jesus is calling	65
On to Victory	158
Speed Thy coming	150
The Gospel's Triumph	4
We'll take the World for Jesus	152

Occasional.

A happy New Year	162
By cool Siloam's shady Rill (Funereal)	17
National Hymn	135
Resting in the Sunlight (Funereal)	86
The Book of the New Year	161
The Hills of Amethyst (Funereal)	47

INDEX OF SUBJECTS.

Praise and Thanksgiving.

	PAGE
All Glory to the Lamb	28
A Song of Joy	82
Holy, Lord God Almighty	9
Hosanna in the Highest	168
My blessed Redeemer	27
Seasons (Thanksgiving)	69
Thanksgiving Hymn	131
Thanks to Thee, our Father	160
The City of God	90
Wonderful Riches	40

Receiving the Saviour

Blessed Assurance	59
Coming to the Cross	79
I heard His call	100
My blessed Redeemer	27
Saviour, Refuge	91
Tell that I'm coming to Jesus	83
Whiter than Snow	52

Temperance.

Sound the Battle-Cry	107
The Armor of God	62
The Christian Soldier	20
The Temperance Banner	95

The Sabbath and Bible.

	PAGE
No Book is like the Bible	103
O Day of Rest	137
Sweet Zion Bells	45
The Sabbath School	108
What do the Bells say?	138

Work and Effort.

At the Setting of the Sun	54
Can the Lord depend on you?	76
Earnest Toilers	6
Follow the Flag of Jesus	67
Higher, ever higher	13
In the King's Highway	34
Jesus calls for Workers	46
Onward, Christian Soldiers	155
Over and over again	120
Practice what you preach	18
Scatter Sunshine and Gladness	42
Something every Day	104
Sowing Seeds of Good or Ill	56
Stand up for Jesus	148
The Middle of the King's Highway	38
The Armor of God	62
The Christian Soldier	20
The Toilers' Song	36
Watch and pray	88

INDEX OF FAMILIAR HYMNS.

Abide with me! Fast falls the eventide	81	Lord, I hear of showers of blessing	139
Alas! and did my Saviour bleed	85	Mary to the Saviour's tomb	179
All hail the power of Jesus' name	97	My faith looks up to Thee	93
Blest be the tie that binds	37	O day of rest and gladness	137
By cool Siloam's shady rill	17	O, think of a home over there	63
Christ, the Lord, is risen to-day	171	O what amazing words of grace	101
Come Thou Almighty King	133	Praise God from whom all blessings	183
Fade, fade, each earthly joy	105	Rock of Ages, cleft for me	159
Hark! from the midnight hills around	169	Silently the shades of ev'ning	151
Holy, holy, holy! Lord God Almighty	9	Sun of my soul, Thou Saviour dear	163
I am coming to the cross	79	The flow'ry spring at Thy command	69
Jesus, refuge of my soul	51	The great Physician now is near	121
Jesus, Saviour, pilot me	33	Unfurl the temp'rance banner	95
Joy to the world, the Lord is come	175	What a Friend we have in Jesus	55
Just as I am, without one plea	113	Work, for the night is coming	115